a kiss is
still a kiss

a kiss is
still a kiss

celebrating the moments that
make marriage last

laura jensen walker

Revell

Grand Rapids, Michigan

Published by Fleming H. Revell
a division of Baker Publishing Group
P.O. Box 6287, Grand Rapids, MI 49516-6287

Printed in the United States of America

Published in association with the literary agency of Alive Communications, Inc.,
7680 Goddard Street, Suite 200, Colorado Springs, Colorado 80920.

Library of Congress Cataloging-in-Publication Data
Walker, Laura Jensen.
    A kiss is still a kiss : celebrating the moments that make marriage last /
Laura Jensen Walker.
        p.   cm.
    Includes bibliographical references.
    ISBN 0-8007-5895-1
    1. Marriage. 2. Marriage—Humor. 3. Married people—Psychology.
4. Marriage—Religious aspects–Christianity. I. Title.
HQ734.W189 2005
306.81—dc22   2004027865

For my beloved husband, Michael: friend, lover, soul mate, confidant, dream sharer, and the most artistic person I've ever known. I'd marry you all over again, honey. "Shut the door."

Love is like a violin. The music may stop now and then, but the strings remain forever.

June Masters Bacher

Contents

Foreword

Sometime in the mid-1950s a secret government experiment went completely awry, and in a bizarre process that researchers are still trying to understand, the lunatic personality of Carol Burnett was cross-pollinated with the DNA of Phyllis Diller. The result was Laura Jensen Walker.

Laura burst onto the writing scene with her first nonfiction work, *Dated Jekyll, Married Hyde*. This title was not a poke at her husband, Michael. On the contrary, as the book made abundantly clear, it was Laura who began as the kindly and proper Jekyll and was subsequently revealed as, well, not exactly Hyde. It was more like Daffy Duck.

After absorbing a dose of Laura's material, it is common for readers to begin mumbling to themselves.

9

"She didn't . . . ," they will mutter.

"Surely, she had to have made that up . . . ," they will exclaim.

"No one could possibly be so utterly daft . . ."

Oh, but she is. And more so. It is all true. That is why her eminently patient spouse, Michael, is so worthy of our admiration and so needful of our deepest intercessory prayers. Especially when he is driving. In England. On the wrong side of the road. With her.

Laura is a complex mix of mirth, lunacy, and ridiculous frivolity tempered by depth, insight, and suffering. It is an odd combination. But it works, because it is real.

Laura has survived a vicious bout with cancer. She endured chemotherapy, debilitating physical weakness, and reconstructive surgery. It was her deep faith, coupled with her irrepressible sense of humor, that helped her survive.

She has earned the right to be taken seriously, even though she is a preposterous nutcase, a modern Lucille Ball.

This madcap woman, with her chocolate obsession, her devotion to old movies, and her numerous and completely unchecked quirks, has some things to teach us about life, love, and hanging wallpaper as a couple (it is a short lesson— "don't").

If you want a serious book about marriage or expert advice on a problematic relationship, then this is *not* the book you are looking for.

This is a peek inside the life of a married couple who, while unique, are every man and every woman. You will see yourself in these pages. Guys cannot help but relate to Michael, because he is speaking the very words we have spoken. Women will empathize with Laura, because they had *exactly* the same thought about that situation when it came up in their relationship. Uncanny. And spooky.

Surely, we aren't all as daft as . . . ?

Maybe we are.

As I see the give-and-take of love worked out in the lives of Michael and Laura, I cannot help but see the hand of God. Only he could have dreamed up this wonderful, frustrating, blissful, painful, utterly complex thing we call marriage.

He calls us to commit ourselves to another person, in good times and in bad times, come what may. And then he sets about using our spouse, with all of his or her associated quirks, habits, traits, hopes, and fears, to fashion us into a being more to God's liking. It is in marriage, more than any other relationship, that we learn to sacrifice, to truly love, to be strong when we'd rather be weak, to press on when we'd rather quit, to lay down our life for our partner, our soul mate, our best friend. Hang on for a wild ride.

Dave Meurer, author of *Good Spousekeepinig*

# Introduction

A happy marriage is a long conversation

which always seems too short.

Andre Maurois

First things first.

I'm not *Dr.* Laura—she's thin, blonde, and Jewish, and I'm, well . . . not. All we have in common is the same first name and the fact that we both write books. I'm not a marriage counselor, nor do I pretend, or even want, to be.

Although I sure wouldn't mind her income.

But being a therapist or counselor is a huge responsibility, and I'm not up for the task. Especially since I didn't even take Psych 101 in college, for goodness' sake.

That's why I was so surprised several years ago after I wrote my first humor book, *Dated Jekyll, Married Hyde*, when I was a guest on a LIVE national call-in radio show, and the host expected me to offer answers and how-to solutions ON THE AIR to a poor, sobbing, and very hurting woman whose marriage was in shambles.

Clearly, the host hadn't read my funny, non-how-to book. (Now, having done a zillion radio interviews over the years, I understand. There often isn't time for hosts to do so, what with all the books they have to read and guests they have to interview.)

But back then I assumed they always did.

And back then I also had no clue that just because I wrote a book with *marriage* in the title, I was automatically rendered an expert on the subject.

A marriage expert.

Even though I'd been married only five years.

And even though it was a humor book.

Hmm. Wonder if Erma Bombeck ever ran into that problem?

Meanwhile, there I was live on a national radio show, expected to provide comfort and some magic marital solution

14

to this unhappy, heartbroken woman. Can you say, in over my head?

I shot a quick "Help, Lord!" heavenward, then thankfully remembered some pastoral advice Michael and I had received in premarital counseling on the very subject the woman was asking about, which I was able to share with her. I also prayed for her and recommended she seek professional help from her pastor or a marriage counselor.

Whew. Saved by the prayer.

That's why I wanted to announce right up front that I'm no marriage counselor. I'm simply a writer, humorist, and imperfect wife who's been—most of the time, except for when he drives me crazy—happily married for nearly fifteen years to a sweet, talented, but imperfect husband, Michael.

So if you're reading this book, hoping to find the answers to all your serious marital problems, stop right now and go make an appointment with a psychologist, a marriage counselor, or your local pastor instead.

Okay, now that we've got that important disclaimer out of the way, you can continue reading—especially if you've been married awhile and would like to know that you're not alone when you get frustrated with your spouse's little idiosyncrasies and habits and want to run screaming from the room when he misunderstands you for the seventh time this weekend.

Or leaves the kitchen a mess after making a snack.

Or balks at going to visit your great aunt Louella this Sunday because there's a game on.

He can't help it. He's from a different planet. Remember? And so are you. (Sure wish I'd been the one to pen that novel concept.) But it sure is nice when those planets collide, isn't it? Well, most of the time anyway.

In these pages you'll find stories—some funny, some touching—from my marriage and the marriages of other couples I interviewed, as well as nuggets of marital wisdom from people who've already "been there, done that" and paved the way for the rest of us on the way to wedded bliss. So hold on to your wedding rings and join me on this fun, wonderful adventure we call "happily ever after"—even when the man makes you crazy.

And remember, God said, "It is not good for the man to be alone." The same holds true for women.

> Marrying a man is like buying something you've
> been admiring for a long time in a shop window.
> You may love it when you get it home, but it
> doesn't always go with everything else.
>
> *Jean Kerr*

1
Becoming One (Another)

Love is what you've been through with somebody.

James Thurber

They say the longer a couple is married, the more they start to look like each other. Well, after close to fifteen years of marriage, that's certainly not the case for Michael and me.

Except for our matching sumo-wrestler tummies. And mustaches. (Although his is darker and thicker than mine—the mustache, I mean.) The day I start growing a beard is when I'll really start to worry. And call my doctor for hormones.

17

Although my husband and I don't look alike, we certainly have *become* more alike over the years—in many, many ways. I wish I could say we've picked up each other's good attributes, but mostly it's the bad habits or qualities.

For instance, I've always had a problem with loud or incessant noise. Which is why I never listen to commercials—ever notice how the sound INCREASES with commercials?—and always hit the mute button the moment they come on. Or when I pull up to a stoplight and the car next to me has its steady, thumping bass turned up as loud as it can go. That's when the windows go up and *Madame Butterfly* goes on.

But it's the repetitive, incessant little noises around the house that really get to me. Like air conditioners, humming refrigerators, or thumping dishwashers. (Although, since we haven't had a dishwasher in nearly a decade, I only hear that particular noise when I visit other people's homes.)

Besides, rumor has it that they make dishwashers today that are virtually silent. I'll let you know when we remodel our kitchen. This year, Lord willing.

Also, because our house doesn't have dual-pane windows yet and isn't insulated (*next* year's remodeling efforts, Lord willing), I hear the steady thump, thump, thump of the neighbor boys playing basketball right outside my living room window on an almost daily basis.

I keep wondering why they can't play Nerf basketball.

a kiss is still a kiss

Something about the whole bounce and dribble thing, I guess.

But I digress.

My noise annoyance, which was at its zenith during the PMS years, has abated somewhat, thanks to menopause.

Now Michael has it.

Noise annoyance, I mean. Not menopause.

And his biggest noise pet peeve is ticking clocks. Especially during the night when he's trying to sleep. He's been known to leap out of bed snarling, "TICK, TICK, TICK!" and grab all the clocks within earshot and shove them in the linen closet, deep in the center of a stack of towels. Only then can he get some sleep.

> *My noise annoyance, which was at its zenith during the PMS years, has abated somewhat, thanks to menopause.*

I've learned.

Now we've switched to digital alarm clocks and removed the batteries from the pretty, decorative clocks in the part of the house near the bedroom.

Speaking of alarm clocks . . . There's one way we have NOT become one, and that's Michael's morning alarm clock ritual.

We must have the most offensive, loud, and ANGRY alarm

clock on the planet. When it assaults me in the morning with its shrill, insistent EEEEA, EEEEA, EEEEA, I do one of two things—leap clear out of bed in shocked awakening or clap my hands on my ears and burrow under my pillow as Michael fumbles to hit the snooze button. (The alarm's on his side of the bed because he's the one who has to get up and drive to work. My work is just a short walk down the hall.)

Ten minutes later, the EEEEA, EEEEA, EEEEA begins again. And Michael hits the snooze button.

Ten minutes later, again. And again with the snooze button.

By this time I'm ready to rip apart either the alarm or my husband.

The last several months, thankfully—probably in self-defense—my internal alarm clock goes off before Michael's electronic one, and I leap out of bed and head down the hall to my office a full half hour before his morning alarm ritual.

Saved by the biological clock.

In addition to noise irritation (what I dubbed "pimsnee," for PMS Noise Irritation), Michael's ability to withstand the heat has also changed over the years.

When I met my California boy, he loved scorching Sacramento summers and the blazing sun, while I, on the other hand, tried to stay as far away from it as possible—barricading myself in air-conditioned buildings and venturing out only to get in the car and drive to important destinations.

Like chocolate runs.

Now, after more than a decade of marriage, Michael can't handle the heat either. It's called aging. Or becoming one.

Or spending eight hours a day in a freezing, air-conditioned building.

I've also become a bit more like my husband over the years.

Michael, to most people's surprise, since he's a former actor, is an introvert. He can be talkative and outgoing onstage before an audience of thousands—but that's when he's playing a part.

Offstage, if you put him in a room with thousands of people—or more than just a handful—he's in agony. He's not a talker. My sweetheart's even uncomfortable with small talk. Although one place this doesn't hold true is in the grocery checkout line. There, for some reason, he feels comfortable telling our life story—vacation plans, remodeling ideas, plumbing problems—to the checker.

While I just want to grab my groceries and go. Which is a little odd because, of the two of us, I'm the extrovert. Guess it's my Jekyll/Hyde personality coming out again.

Before Michael and I met, I frolicked frequently in the extrovert arena. Especially in my singles days. I was always the life of the party or the "class clown"—performing silly skits, organizing social events, bantering (aka flirting, but intelligently) back and forth with the guys.

Needing, wanting to be noticed—especially by any potential Mr. Rights.

But that wasn't the case in my younger days. In childhood, I started out as an introvert—a quiet little girl with her nose always in a book. Yet I was also a fearless tomboy—preferring to play with trucks or build forts with the boy across the street rather than play with dolls.

The nose in the book part hasn't changed a bit. I'd still rather be reading than just about anything. But the tomboy part has pretty much vanished. In many ways, I've become quite the "girly girl," liking teacups and lace, hating dirt and mice, and being not the least bit interested in playing with trucks.

Marriage to Michael, or simply the passing of time and growing up and older, has made me meander across both the "ex" and the "in" sides of that "trovert" line.

The extrovert part of me is the speaker who talks to large crowds without getting nervous, feels completely comfortable during a live TV interview, and is ultracompetitive in board games—especially Trivial Pursuit.

The introvert part of me is the voracious reader and writer who works at home alone all day long and deliberately doesn't venture out to crowded events—like festivals, concerts, fairs, and Disneyland. I much prefer the home-court advantage and am quite content to savor my excitement from the comfort of my wingback chair.

That's another way Michael and I have become more alike over the years, but in a good way—we're both homebodies now.

I've been working at home for several years, but it took some time to make the adjustment from being in an office with other people to talk to, take breaks with, or go out to lunch with.

For the first year or so working at home alone, I would get cabin fever—sometimes several times a week. When Michael got home from work at night, I'd be eager to go out—to dinner, grocery shopping, shopping for toilets, ANYwhere after having been cooped up all day.

I was ready to see what was out there in the world again.

And Michael misunderstood. At first he thought it was because I didn't like being home. After being at work all day and then fighting the rush-hour traffic, all Michael wanted in the evening was to escape into our lovely, restful, and quiet home.

Going back out was not high on his to-do list.

This, of course, was a cause for friction in our relationship until we realized what was going on.

Funny what a little thing like communication can do.

Eventually, I started taking a few hours each week as my "get out of the house" free time. Meeting a friend for lunch, browsing through a bookstore, even running errands. It was amazing how much it helped. What was once a daily need to get out turned into a once-a-week need instead.

> ......
> *Funny what a little thing like communication can do.*
> .....

Now I've become more like Michael and enjoy hanging out at home most of the time.

And Michael's become more like me. My husband now appreciates the finer things in life.

When we married, he simply couldn't understand why we needed two sets of dishes—one simple clear glass set for everyday use and a prettier china set for guests and special occasions.

Our china pattern was Blue Willow—a popular pattern that's been around for a couple hundred years (if you look closely, you can see Laura Ingalls and her family using it in reruns of *Little House on the Prairie*). It's that wonderful cobalt blue and white scene complete with doves and a pagoda. There's even a Romeo and Juliet story to it—the boy and girl from feuding families who run away, but rather than killing themselves, they turn into doves and fly away together.

How romantic. (Yes, guys, dishes can be romantic.) I love

a kiss is still a kiss

the story and the dishes, so I brought the pattern to the marriage. And today Michael shares my appreciation for a finely set dinner table complete with linens, candles, and all the pretty accoutrements.

We now have four sets of dishes—and my husband bought two of them.

Including our Old Country Roses, our English bone china. With its lush roses of deep pink and yellow, and its gold trim around the scalloped border, it was one pattern we'd both agreed upon over the years as we window-shopped. But it was an extravagance way beyond our budget. (Yes, Michael not only agrees to window-shop with me for china, silver, and crystal, but he even *enjoys* it. As long as we don't spend too much time in that department.)

One day we were in a local department store that had been bought out by a bigger chain. For fun, we wandered into the china department and saw a sign: "Old Country Roses on clearance!" The new owner didn't carry that pattern, so everything was 75 percent off. Bargain lover Michael couldn't resist, and we got the last four place settings they had.

Trying to be a good, budget-conscious wife, I suggested we buy only two, but Michael, who always sees the big picture, said, "We can't buy just two." Then he recited, "China is used when one entertains guests." Had he been watching a little Martha maybe?

Besides, we'd probably never see a great sale like that again, so he insisted on buying the lot.

Now we have the china of our dreams. And we love it. Both looking at it and *using* it. We don't believe in keeping it on display behind glass in a china cabinet to be used on only very special occasions. Life's too short.

That's why we even eat pizza on the good china.

And one day we plan to visit Stoke-on-Trent, England, to actually see where the china is made. That's another way Michael and I have become more like each other: I introduced him to England and all things British, and now he's more of an Anglophile than me.

Our friends Chris and Steve, who have a year of marriage and five kids on us, say that one of the ways they've become more alike over the years is in their frugality. Several years of marriage and several kids will do that.

Steve was always careful with money, but Chris was a little more carefree with her spending. Today she is the bargain queen.

My sister-in-law Sheri says her husband, Jim, has not become at all like her over the years, but she's definitely become more like him—particularly in her speech habits. Jim is a sweet, fun-loving guy who loves to tease and joke around.

He's even created his own special language, which Sheri now speaks also.

I call it "Jimspeak."

Soon after I met Jim—and before Michael and I were married—he asked me one evening after dinner, "Would you like some Metropolitan?"

"Excuse me?"

"Metropolitan ice cream. You know, the brown, pink, and white kind all in one."

That was my introduction to Jimspeak. He enjoys deliberately changing the names of common things, or the spellings: phy for pie, fude for food, skule for school, and koffee rather than coffee.

Some of it was born out of self-preservation when the kids were little. You know, the typical parent trick of spelling over the kids' heads—except that Jim was never a very good speller. "Want some p-h-y?" he'd ask Sheri. Or if they were out and about and the kids were in the car, if Jim said, "What do you think about having some Marie Callender's?" the kids would bug them until they went to their favorite pie place. So my inventive brother-in-law came up with the idea of calling it Ann Landers instead to throw them off track.

Which worked—for a couple years until they caught on to his tricks.

Although Sheri now speaks Jim's special language, one

area where they have not become one over the years is in the political arena. "It frosts him that I'm listening to Hillary Clinton's book," Sheri the history major said. "The more conservative he gets, the more moderate I get."

Our friend Jan, who's been married to Mike for twelve years, says she's relaxed more over the years.

"I'm not so uptight when I come in the kitchen now and see that the cupboard doors are all left open," Jan said. "Now it's like, *Well, that's what he does.*

"And you know what? I'm a person who comes behind and *closes* the doors," Jan said. "Mike will even say to me, 'Oh, you did this already? I was going to come and do it.'

"So maybe if I gave him a little more time . . ."

Jan thinks it's not so much husbands and wives who look like each other as it is couples and their pets.

"I always get a good laugh when I see couples walking their dogs," she said. "They always look alike." That would apply in their home as well. She and Mike both have blonde hair, and they have a yellow Lab named Frezzi.

Hmm. Michael and I have a white dog, Gracie. Maybe that's why our dark brown hair is getting so gray. Maybe if I dye her, then my hair will turn dark again.

I wonder if Clairol works on fur.

My email pal Roanne, who's been married for thirty-five years, says her husband is bald and she's going gray, so they don't have the looking alike thing going either. But they're definitely finding that they *think* alike; they're always finishing each other's sentences.

"I guess it's the 'twin syndrome' without the umbilical cord," Roanne said.

I can relate. As can most couples, the longer they're married. There's a wonderful spiritual, emotional, and physical bond forged by love, prayer, intimacy, the ups and downs of daily life, a shared history full of laughter, tears, and often, children.

Or in our sumo-wrestler tummies' case, lots of ice cream.

A cord of three strands is not quickly broken.

Ecclesiastes 4:12

2
Her Wants, His Wants

In a successful marriage, there is no such thing as one's way.
There is only the way of both, only the bumpy, dusty,
difficult, but always mutual path.

Phyllis McGinley

When Annette and Randy first got married more than twenty years ago, Annette pictured beautiful weekend breakfasts on china together à la *Bride's* magazine with lots of conversation.

Randy doesn't eat breakfast.

And he's not a big talker either.

Plus, my Texas friend Annette likes to drink from pretty glasses, while her husband prefers a big plastic mug. "Makes for an interesting table setting," she said.

When we first got married, Michael liked plastic too. But I wouldn't allow it on the table. Didn't even want it in the *house*, but I lost that battle.

Now, after all these years, his tastes have become more like mine and he's not as prone to plastic. But I've relaxed considerably as well and don't mind if a colorful plastic glass makes its way to the table these days.

As long as I don't have to drink from it.

Interesting how our differing wants have become more alike over the years. Or how we've learned to be more flexible and accepting of each other's wants and needs.

Unlike many men, Michael's never been a big TV guy. And after growing up in a family where the guys watched televised sports nearly every weekend, I'm more grateful than I can say. In fact, Michael would be happy if we never watched TV—except for favorite old movies on video and DVD, and *Jeopardy.*

But a few years ago, after he turned the big 4-0, something unusual happened. My non-jock husband started getting interested in sports. NBA basketball, in particular. The Sacramento Kings were in the play-offs.

Michael started by watching snippets of the game as he channel surfed. The snippets grew longer as the Kings progressed through the season. After a while, Michael could skip watching the game on TV, but he felt himself strangely drawn to the sports section of the newspaper—something he'd never read before in his life—first just to check out the score, then to read the commentary.

And the TV "snippets" turned into the final quarter of the game. Then the last half.

A little put out at first that my husband was turning into a sports guy

I am not, and never have been, a sports girl.

after all these years, I grudgingly decided to support him in his new hobby—it was, after all, a cheaper midlife crisis than a month-long trip to Europe. Or a red sports car.

One night I even watched a game with him.

And you know what? I got into it! Which shocked everyone who knew me—including my jockette best friend, Lana, and her sports-loving husband, Michael.

I need to stop here for a second and explain something. For those of you who've never met me or read any of my books, there's something you need to know: I am not, and never have been, a sports girl. Not to put too fine a point on it, but basically, I *hate* sports. Always have. Along with loud sports bars. I never got all the screaming and yelling people do at the TV. It always seemed rather juvenile to me.

I'm a quiet artist type, you see—preferring reading, writing, movies, and other more cultural pursuits, which is why my sudden interest in NBA basketball surprised everyone.

Including me.

I didn't know any of these guys' names before, but pretty quickly a little guy with a shaved head and tattoos on his legs named Mike Bibby captured my attention. Little Mike seemed so much smaller than the other guys, yet he was able to turn and scoot around them. He always seemed to be out in the open, and man, could he shoot the ball! One of our team members would be trapped near the basket with an opposing player right on top of him. Then he'd pass to Bibby, far down the court. Swoosh. Three points. No matter how far away he was from the basket, my man Bibby always scored. It was a thing of beauty to watch.

I never got all the screaming and yelling people do at the TV. It always seemed rather juvenile to me.

As the Kings got nearer to winning the series—or whatever it's called—the fan excitement in the Sacramento area grew to a fever pitch. During one particular game, Michael and

I were sitting on the couch, glued to the TV, when we were soon joined by our dog, Gracie. The game was frenzied and exciting, so we barely noticed when Gracie hopped down and went into the other room.

We were getting just a bit too loud for her—Gracie's rather delicate and doesn't like loud noises.

It was a close game, and each basket made for an appropriate exclamation. After a while, Michael got up and left the room too. He went into the office and sat down at the computer to give his ears a break.

But I didn't care—or notice—that I was now all alone in the den. It was a great game.

Come on, defense. "Good block," I hollered at the screen.

Now we've got the ball.

"Come on . . . Come on!"

Darn blockers, or whatever they're called.

"Give the ball to Bibby.

"What's the matter with you? He's wide open! Give the ball to Bibby!"

I was really into the game now.

"GIVE THE BALL TO BIBBY!!!"

I'm sure they heard me next door.

Michael meekly reentered the room. "Honey, do we need to change the channel? You're getting awfully excited."

It was then I realized the power of televised sports.

The Kings made it as far as they could without winning the championship, giving those pesky Lakers the ultimate run for their bonus money. We made it all the way to the tie-breaking overtime in game seven of the western conference finals.

And my Bibby played magnificently, as always.

Then it was over. All over. No more Bibby. Well, not until the next year, anyway.

Fortunately, the pendulum has swung back, and life is more normal again. We're back to watching TV only occasionally, and now Michael likes to read in bed with me.

Rather than turning on the TV most evenings, he'll say, "Honey, let's go in and read."

Works for li'l ol' bookworm me. Thank you, God.

Our home is one of our favorite places to be. But even though we agree on how a room should look, we don't always agree on how to get it there.

Like the redecorating of Michael's craft room—I mean studio.

When we were writing our Christmas book, *God Rest Ye Grumpy Scroogeymen*, together, we moved our desktop computer from my office to his craft room. (For why this was necessary, read the next chapter, "Working Together on Projects without Killing Each Other.") To make room for the computer desk, we had to move Michael's large quilting table out to the garage, which meant less space for crafting.

But, of course, we kept the guest bed in those now-cramped quarters—you never know when you'll have overnight guests.

Soon we were expecting overnight visitors, and the guest room (aka Michael's craft room/computer room), didn't seem so pleasant with the double bed smashed against the wall and boxes of fabric, craft supplies, and even our financial paperwork covering most of the available floor space.

Rather than taking hours to convert the chaos into suitable guest quarters, Michael suggested we just keep the door shut and let our visitors sleep on the hide-a-bed instead. After all, the living room is bed-and-breakfast charming already, and although we'd never used it, the couch does open into a queen-size bed.

Probably fine for one night.

Now, we've had that couch for a good two and a half years. We bought it because we loved the shape and the fabric—a pretty English floral pattern. That it was also a hide-a-bed did not interest us.

Until now.

When we opened up the hide-a-bed, we found the mattress still wrapped in plastic. After removing the plastic, we both lay down on the mattress to try it out. Wow. How comfortable. No bar running across our backs like our old one used to have. And absolutely perfect for those couple times a year when we have sleepover guests.

Which brings us back to Michael's room and the guest bed.

Inspired by a book about simplifying your life so you can follow your dreams, Michael decided to reclaim his craft room from the clutter bugs. The guest bed was now redundant, and therefore unnecessary, so it was taken away and replaced with a four-drawer filing cabinet, a clear plastic storage bin unit, and a new, more compact utility table.

Much more interested in function than form, Michael was chomping at the bit to get started creating things with his art. While I, on the other hand, couldn't wait for him to redecorate the room. It's not that I wanted everything cleaned up already. I just wanted it to be pretty.

It's not that I wanted everything cleaned up already, I just wanted it to be pretty.

So I went in and "helped" him.

We added a shelf unit to one wall, which meant several of his pictures and paintings now needed to be moved or adjusted. I had a great time with the redecorating, and we got the major pieces all in place. There were still several boxes on the floor to be gone through and papers to be filed or pitched, which I was eager to help him do.

That's when Michael looked over at me and plaintively said, "Honey, I want to do *my* art."

Initially miffed that he no longer wanted my help, I left to go do other projects and then head to bed. When I awoke the next morning, I was amazed to see my husband's new creation in progress: an exquisite quilted wall hanging of a descending dove—the Holy Spirit—for our church. The background, pieced together out of two-inch squares of different colored fabric, looks like an Impressionist painting.

Wow.

So what if the room isn't totally organized yet? The main thing is that my honey is creating again and happy.

Besides, there's always next weekend.

When shopping for a house, my friend Annette, like me, needs cute.

"Cute is way more important to me than practical," Annette said. "So what if the floor's uneven or there are no electrical outlets in the master bath? It's got glass-front cabinets in the kitchen and a cranberry-red front door."

Preach it, sister.

Guess that's why God had us marry more practical-minded men. Even though their sleeping habits are so different from ours.

The first few years of our marriage, Michael and I had a

double bed because he really likes to snuggle and wanted to be as close to me as possible.

I like to snuggle too, but not when I'm ready to go to sleep. Then I need my space. Only problem was, I'm apparently an active sleeper.

I say "apparently" because I don't know this firsthand. Shortly after my head hits the pillow, I'm out for the night.

But I have pretty vivid dreams—influenced by movies I watch or books I read. For years and years, I would dream that the Nazis were after me. (*The Diary of Anne Frank* made a huge impression on me. Plus, I paid a memorable visit to the Dachau concentration camp when I was stationed in Germany.)

The dream was always the same. Faceless Nazis in heavy boots running up the stairs and discovering my hiding place in the attic, and me jumping from roof to roof to escape and then running up and down apartment stairways, knocking on doors, seeking refuge. Sometimes a kind soul would take me in and offer sanctuary, but always the Nazis would eventually find me.

And as they grabbed me, I'd break away and jump off the roof—which often woke me up. But apparently, I thrashed and kicked wildly about while trying to escape their grasp.

And Michael bore the brunt of my kicking. One night

he had to shake me awake and say, "Laura, stop kicking me. I'm not the Nazis."

Poor Michael. We traded in the cozy double bed for a nice big king-size shortly thereafter. Now we're both happy. We'll snuggle for a while and then return to our opposite sides of the bed for sleeping. And I'm happy to report that the Nazi nightmares have stopped.

Annette and Randy have had some sleep struggles over the years as well. Or in their case, it's more like waking-up struggles.

"I'm a morning person; he's not," Annette said. "But over the years I've adapted to Randy's style of mornings. Basically, we do our morning stuff in total silence. No radio, no TV, and certainly no conversation. We don't even turn on lights. Instead, we grope around in the dark."

It took Annette a while to get used to the latter. "But now it seems very odd to me when we're visiting friends or hosting overnight guests that they actually turn lights on and talk before 9 a.m.," she said.

I can vouch for that. When Annette came out to visit me in California, she didn't know how to act when I bounced out of bed at 7:30, opened all the blinds, and began chattering away about our plans for the day.

Good thing Randy stayed behind in Texas.

Her Wants, His Wants ● ● ● ●

Marriage was ordained for a remedy and to
increase the world and for the man to help the
woman and the woman the man,
with all love and kindness.

William Tyndale

a kiss is still a kiss

3

Working Together on Projects without Killing Each Other

A working girl is one who quit her job to get married.

My husband and I know better than to wallpaper together. Ever.

We tried it—once. Can you say, quickest way to Judge Judy?

That's because Michael's meticulous—always measuring

43

and marking, cutting just so, and taking his time to make sure everything's absolutely perfect. (When he read this, he disagreed with me. "Not absolutely perfect, honey. I'm not a perfectionist. Just *reasonably* perfect.")

Whatever. Reasonable or absolute, I'm neither. I'm the impatient, slap-it and wrap-it girl, in a hurry to get done and move on to something else.

This applies to most areas of our life together, particularly projects around the house. However, for some reason—even after more than a decade of marriage, mind you—I thought it would be different when we wrote our first book together—*God Rest Ye Grumpy Scroogeymen.*

When we began, Michael and I had fantasies of collaborating on many more books as husband and wife—happily envisioning ourselves as the next Brock and Bodie Thoene. But I have a funny feeling those fantasies may never become reality.

Unless one of us changes.

We barely survived the collaborative process, you see.

It all began the day Michael sat down next to me in my office.

First, you need to know that I'm a woman who needs her personal space, or as Virginia Woolf so eloquently put it, "a room of [her] own."

As I typed furiously away on my laptop, out of the corner

of my eye I could see Michael—sitting in front of the desktop computer, staring at it and thinking.

Just sitting there. Breathing.

It was enough to drive a person crazy. Especially this person.

I could hear every breath he took, every shift in his chair, every twitch of his eye. And it was deafening.

Finally, when I couldn't stand it any longer, I suggested we go out to dinner. I treated Michael to a meal at one of his favorite Mexican restaurants, then waited until just the right moment— after he'd polished off his chicken fajitas—to broach the subject with my sensitive husband.

> *I could hear every breath he took, every shift in his chair, every twitch of his eye. And it was deafening.*

"Honey, I don't want you to get upset, but I have something I need to share with you," I began nervously.

Michael paled, flashing back to breast cancer and thinking I'd found another lump.

But I quickly reassured him. "No, no, it's nothing like that."

Deep breath. "I love you, honey, but I need you out of my office. I just can't work in the same room with you," I said. "Please don't be hurt."

He wasn't in the least. What he was was relieved that it wasn't something serious.

The next morning Michael went to an appointment with a massage therapist to work out the kinks in his back and neck. When he came home, I was in the middle of a house reorganization and made him help me move the heavy furniture, thereby effectively negating the sixty bucks he'd just spent at the masseuse.

Aside from messing up his massage, it was the smartest thing we ever did. Now we each had separate rooms to work in, and we could leave each other alone to do our own thing.

But we still had very different working styles. Particularly as they relate to writing.

I majored in journalism at college and have been writing for years. And thanks to my journalism background, I write really fast and work best under the pressure of a deadline.

Not Michael.

Deadlines—at least in this new artistic venue of writing—stress him out. He's very methodical and measured and thinks about things for a long time before he does them.

Michael's a thoughtful guy, which is something most women want in a man. Before he sat down to write one

46

word of his first book, he'd been thinking for weeks and weeks—maybe even months—about what he wanted to say. So by the time he began typing, he had a clear direction in his head.

And his first draft was pretty close to final.

Not me.

I start with a vague, general idea of what I want to do, but it isn't until I actually sit down at the computer to write that I know what's going to happen. My first drafts are a mess—a hodgepodge of "blah, blah, blahs" and fill in the blanks later. And far from final.

Not to put it too graphically (please don't read this while you're eating), but one day Michael said to me, "When you write, you throw up on the page and then just pick out the good chunks."

He's right—although I wouldn't have put it quite that way. That's a guy thing.

When I sit down at the keyboard, my fingers fly . . . I think fast, talk fast, and type fast—a hundred words a minute, thank you very much.

Michael's the total opposite. He's my slow-moving, slow-talking man.

A couple months after he'd begun writing, he said to me, "Um, honey, have you started working on your chapters yet?"

"Nope. But don't worry. I will."

A few weeks later, Michael, who by now had five or six chapters already written, compared to my ZERO, said, "Um, honey. Don't you think you'd better get started writing?"

"Not yet, dear. I'm still busy working on the publicity and promotion on the last book—I have to wrap that up first. Not to worry though, darling, I never miss a deadline. Besides," I said with a gracious smile, "I've done this before."

Michael would spend six or seven hours writing his first draft of a chapter, while I'd spend forty-five minutes. Then we'd swap chapters and read each other's work.

Now, because I'm also an editor with a screaming aversion to misspelled words—on the college newspaper they nicknamed me the "human dictionary"—when I sat down to read Michael's work for the first time, I automatically corrected punctuation, typos, and misspelled words as I read.

With a red pen.

When I handed the chapters back to Michael, he was crushed.

"You bled all over the page," he said.

"But that doesn't mean I didn't like it."

"Couldn't prove it by me."

"No, honey, look. It's mostly typos and punctuation, that's all. See? The content's wonderful."

And it was. Thanks to all the thinking and planning Michael had done ahead of time, his first draft was pretty much final. And fabulous.

I hadn't realized what a good writer my husband is.

But I'd also forgotten what it's like when you write your first book, how sensitive you are to any hint of criticism, when I slashed through his pages with red ink.

Our editor and friend offered a gentle suggestion: "Use a blue pen. It makes all the difference."

So I did. And then I showed Michael *my* first draft. And my husband didn't know how to tell me, "There's nothing here that ties this all together. It's not cohesive. It's just a bunch of notes."

"Yeah. So what's your point?"

We quickly learned. Different people, different writing styles. And different methods of working.

But once we got past that learning curve of writing together, ultimately, we were successful in working together on the book, and the end result is better than what either of us could have written alone.

So watch out, Brock and Bodie . . .

Several years ago, my aunt Sharon and uncle Jim had new carpet laid upstairs. Unfortunately, once the carpet was down, the doors didn't fit anymore—it was too snug with the raised carpet. So together they tried to get the bedroom door off to sand it down to fit. After several tense minutes of getting in the way, Sharon decided to go downstairs and keep busy.

"Jimmy used the sander and afterward discovered he'd done the top of the door, not the bottom," Sharon said. "It's still like that today."

I can relate.

There are a couple projects Michael's started and never finished.

Like the front screen door—the spring-back thingy at the top never got put on, so it just slams wide open and stays that way until one of us pulls it shut again. But that's okay. I don't mind. It still looks good and works well, so that works for me.

Especially the looking good part—that's what's most important in my book.

And the chain-link fence for the dog run. There are these stabilizing clips that are supposed to go along the top of the fence, but the day Michael and his brother put the fence up, it was really hot, so he decided to finish that later.

Six years later it's still not done. But again, it doesn't bother me. The fence is up, it's doing the job it's supposed to do, so what's the problem?

Michael didn't know this when we were dating, but I'm the daughter of the queen of clean. Just call me Princess Clean. Except when I'm on deadline. Then dishes pile up in the sink, beds don't get made, rooms don't get dusted or vacuumed, and my office becomes a minefield one must enter at his or her own risk.

Michael may be my prince, but he's definitely not the prince of clean. For years, it amazed me that my artistic, creative husband, who is such a perfectionist in almost everything he does, whether it's quilting, painting, wallpapering, gardening, whatever, could be such a—how can I put this delicately?—slob.

No, wait. That's a little too harsh. He's really not a slob. He's just kind of messy. Especially when it comes to cleaning up after himself in the kitchen.

Michael's a terrific cook. His lasagna is the best I've ever had. Ditto on his spaghetti, chili, mashed potatoes—skins on, natch—and carrot cake. But he's not too big on the whole clean-up aspect.

Picture a white stove and bubbling tomato sauce.

My sweetie always tries to wipe up, and he usually manages

to get the large blobs of tomato, but he never seems to see the countless other red flecks peppering the top of the stove, utensil caddy, or shiny silver teakettle.

So I always come behind him and scrub them off.

Then there's his breakfast. Often Michael likes to make toast or a bagel in the morning before he goes to work. He's always careful to set down a paper towel on the cutting board to make his breakfast.

But when he leaves for work, he also leaves the crumby paper towel behind on the counter. And I come behind him and clean it up. If there's one thing I can't stand, it's crumbs on the kitchen counter.

But my cleaning habits have nothing on my mom, the queen of clean.

Mom's from the clean-as-you-go school. And it drives Michael crazy. One year, the first Thanksgiving after my stepfather died, she asked Michael to come cook the Thanksgiving turkey in her new apartment.

He was happy to oblige.

Only problem was, every time he turned around, she was picking up after him. He'd stir the gravy and set the spoon down for a moment. And when he turned around to pick it up, it was gone. Mom had already washed it and put it away.

Not putting things away—particularly his clothes—is a trait of my brother-in-law Jim, his wife, Sheri, tells me.

"He has a habit of dropping clothes wherever he wants. Like his bathrobe," Sheri said. "When we were first married and he did this, I thought, *Surely he's just oblivious to the fact that you don't do that, and he'll pick it up.*"

But he didn't. And neither did Sheri.

In time, she was able to train her new husband, however. "If he didn't pick it up and put it in the dirty clothes, it didn't get washed," Sheri said. "Very simple."

Jim was a quick study.

My friend Marianne says one must be very specific when talking to a husband about laundry.

"Asking him to put a load of clothes in the washer is just that," Marianne said. "I guess I forgot to mention to put the soap in and turn the machine on too. Silly me. When I finally got across all the how-tos of the washer, I then should have remembered to remind him that when it is finished, one must actually move the clothes to the dryer and turn it on. Forget the lint trap."

"Keep in mind that this is a man who can build almost anything," Marianne said. "Tony can take apart a car and put it back together. But this is the same man who becomes a bumbling mess when face-to-face with a basket of dirty clothes. He actually told his mother about the 'magic laundry basket' in our room. He puts clothes in one day, and the next day those same clothes appear folded in his drawer. Imagine that!"

Now I'll give Tony equal time and let him tell his side of the story.

"One day I was telling my mom how great my wife is," Tony recalled. "I told her that my wife is so efficient that it's as if we have a magic laundry basket. I don't know how she does it, but my clothes are always clean and put away. It's great!"

Laundry is a perplexing subject to Tony. "If a T-shirt has printing on it, is it white or mixed?" he wanted to know. "How about socks with little flowers on them? And what is up with people throwing stuff like wet dishrags in the washer? Am I really supposed to touch that nasty thing or just throw the next load in on top of it?"

The laundry-impaired Tony also complains that the washer never finishes when expected. "It always seems to be this suspended state of in-between cycles that begin and end by a random time-span generator," he said. "When I check to see if the load is finished, it's always just sitting there, a gaping tub of mashed clothes—like carnival cyclone riders permanently stuck to the sides of the spinning wall.

"I'm not sticking my hands in there until I disconnect the power," he declared.

"And if I did that, it would never finish. By then it's time for a nap anyway."

Tony insists that his clothes are disappearing—a little bit at a time. "Where do you think all that lint comes from?" he asked. "Washers don't eat socks. Lint traps suck them up one little thread at a time until a blanket of soft fuzz has covered the screen.

"Did you ever wonder how thick you could get that lint? I once put all the socks in the house in the dryer for four hours," Tony said. "Marianne wasn't home during this experiment, but she knew. Don't ask me how, but she did.

"Now I don't go near the thing.

"But my wife, she has that stuff nailed," he said proudly. "If it were left up to me, everything we owned would be a shade of pink.

"We're a good match," Tony said. "She sends me to my mother in Ohio twice a year for a couple weeks. Her house stays neat, and she can eat out every day. I come home with all my laundry clean (I don't understand my mother's machines any better), and the love story starts all over again."

My Ohio friend Joyce and her husband, Dan, have come up with a novel solution to working together on projects. "When he has a project planned, I get in the van and go to the mall," Joyce said.

"I stay away twice as long as I think the project should take."

Maybe I should take a page from Joyce's book.

> Marriage is not just spiritual communion and passionate embraces; marriage is also three meals a day, sharing the workload and remembering to carry out the trash.
>
> *Dr. Joyce Brothers*

a kiss is still a kiss

4
Practicing the KISS Principle

Often the difference between a successful marriage
and a mediocre one consists of leaving about
three or four things a day unsaid.

Harlan Miller

Michael, like most men—okay, I don't want to be accused of being sexist here, so I'll say "many" instead. Michael, like *many* men, has a short attention span.

Especially when it comes to talking.

Or rather, listening. To me. As I go on and on about something—especially pertaining to our relationship or a disagreement we may have had.

When my darling and I have a misunderstanding or argument, as a woman, I always want to *explain* my position. Particularly when I don't feel that he understands where I'm coming from.

A pet peeve of mine is when I'm explaining and he interjects something.

"Honey, please don't interrupt. I'm trying to have a conversation with you."

"I'm not interrupting. I'm letting you know I understand so we can move forward with this discussion," he says. "The bottom line is that you feel this way, right?" Impatient fidgeting in chair and longing look at office door. "So can I get back to what I was doing now?"

"Yes, that is the bottom line, dear, but what I need you to know is that when I said this, what I *meant* was that, and this is how I felt about it. And when you said such and such, what I thought you were saying was this and that . . ."

Along about now, for some reason, Michael gets this pained expression on his face, and I can *see* him lose interest and shut down before my eyes, which only frustrates me more.

Until I learned the KISS principle, that is. (Keep it short,

a kiss is still a kiss

sweetheart.) I've discovered that if I try to minimize my discussion to, say, less than ten minutes, and cut to the heart of the matter as soon as possible, my husband's happier.

And we don't have another fight about my female need to relate and talk at length about our disagreement or difference of opinion.

That's why over the years (for the most part) I've learned that if I really need to work through everything I'm feeling and to discuss every single aspect and nuance of our argument, it's best to go to one of my girlfriends.

However, there are still times I forget and put Michael through the discussion wringer. I blame it on midlife—but also that feminine need to share and talk. And talk. And talk. Especially if I think I'm right.

One thing Michael hates more than anything is to talk. And talk. And talk a subject to death. Or rather, to have to listen when I talk and talk and talk. Particularly if he doesn't feel we're making any progress.

My aunt Char understands where I'm coming from. "If I knew that I was without a doubt 100 percent right, then I wanted my husband to *understand* my rightness," she said.

Her husband, Wayne, whom she was married to for more than twenty-five years, was more passive and didn't like to argue.

"My oldest stepson always called us Laurel and Hardy," Char said. "We never fought, but we would bicker."

Randy and Annette don't fight either.

"We both hate conflict, so we just sweep it under the rug," my Texas girlfriend said. "We just learn to live with stuff. It's probably not particularly healthy, but it works for us."

Annette says she's often thought they should have a little more discussion, and once, after seeing a movie with a loud, colorful couple who really hashed things out, she suggested to Randy, "Maybe it would be better if we were more like that."

But her husband disagreed with a horrified "Oh no."

"He sees no point in getting loud," Annette said. "He just hates it."

For the most part, the couple gets along very well.

"I didn't want to be a bossy wife at all," my gracious Southern friend said, "so I learned very quickly to adapt. I always thought bossiness was really unattractive, and it's so important to be attractive."

"Women talk to relate, and men talk to relate too—like the score of the Kings game or the fact that we're out of mayonnaise," said my new writing pal Christie. "Women glean knowledge from context, so naturally, we provide full details in all their glory. And we expect rich details in return—until

a kiss is still a kiss

we've been married long enough to learn that men do not love this."

This was firmly brought home to Christie the day she expectantly queried her husband about a wedding he'd gone to without her.

"So how was it?" Christie asked, wanting the 411 on colors and decorations, the bride's dress, the guest list, who was in the wedding party, the location, if there was any dancing, and what the food, including the cake, was like.

"Fine," Greg replied.

Christie and Greg fondly refer to their polar communication styles as *Roots*—as in the tome by Alex Haley—for her and *Cliffs Notes* for him.

"He does get very wordy and excited occasionally," Christie admitted, "but it's usually over something I want the quick and dirty version of. Like his camera equipment."

Greg knows that his wife loves photographs and scrapbooking, but she says that when he started in about the apertures, F-stops, exposure value ranges, and gray cards on his new camera, her eyes glazed over.

"He trailed off uncertainly, and I wanted to say, 'I just want a stunning finished product. I don't care about a lesson on how to get it, starting with, "On the first day, God created light,"'" Christie recalled. "Instead, I offered, 'That's nice, honey.'

"I could finally understand how men must feel."

Roanne, another email pal of mine, married very young and said that early on in their marriage, she and her husband hadn't learned the "don't sweat the small stuff" rule, so they had many arguments in the beginning.

"The second week of our marriage, we got into it again over something (I don't really remember what)," Roanne said, "and I decided I was 'going home.'"

So she yanked out a suitcase and carefully started packing her clothes. Her husband let her get so far, then grabbed her clothes and threw them on the bed. Roanne picked them up, folded them, and put them back in the suitcase. He grabbed them again and threw them back on the bed.

"This went back and forth for a while until we were both doubled over laughing," Roanne recalled. "Of course, I wound up staying, and we both completely forgot what the squabble was about."

My seventy-something friend June, who was married forty-two years before her husband, Red, passed away, said the biggest crises in her marriage were when Red came home and informed her he'd just bought a new truck, the boat, a car.

"All separate incidences," June said. "There never was a

discussion with me, just 'You're such a good money manager, and I know you'll see we get it paid for.'

"The time came when I picked up the pre-purchase clues," she recalled. "He'd say, 'So-and-so just got a new Dodge pickup; pretty good on gas and good out in the desert or on mountain roads.' 'So-and-so just got this great little boat, and his kids are water-skiing. His wife wants to learn too. They have a great time together. He invited us to meet them and try out the boat.'

"BIG-TIME WARNINGS. Time for me to be prepared to review our income and financial output with him and strongly emphasize why we couldn't afford those purchases," June recalled. "Mostly, I lost. For a number of years I did a lot of retreating. Somehow the bills were paid and we survived. We did have some enjoyable times with the truck and the boat, and in time, we worked out the buying process. The good memories outlive the not-so-good ones, and I'm grateful for that."

The KISS principle isn't only about keeping it short, sweetheart. It's also about kissing and making up after a fight.

My uncle Jim, who's been married to my aunt Sharon for forty-three years, is a mostly quiet fighter.

"He won't say a word," said Sharon. "He'll go to another

part of the house where he doesn't want to be seen or heard, and of course I follow right behind him, either still finishing the argument or screaming at him or saying, 'What happened here? How did we get to this point?'"

The KISS principle isn't only about keeping it short, sweetheart. It's also about kissing and making up after a fight.

Jim's response? "I don't want to talk about it."

"If he feels he was at fault, he'll still keep up his stubbornness," Sharon said, "and then two or three hours later, he'll come up and say, 'Well, I'm sorry too,' and throw me a kiss and say, 'Let's get over it.'"

Michael does the same thing. Only he prefers to pucker up and plant a big one on my lips after he's hugged me and apologized. Ninety-eight percent of the time I'm receptive, but there have been one or two occasions when I was still so angry (over what, I can't remember now—probably because I felt he didn't listen to me or take my feelings into account) that I've said, "Don't even THINK about touching me right now."

What can I say? It's a girl thing. It passes—once I get to talk it out.

And now for the twentieth anniversary rock fight.

Mark and Cindy, some friends from Kansas, wanted to build a rock walkway between their front and back doors. At 10:30 on their special anniversary night, they were in bed with the lights out when Mark said, "Oh, by the way, we're going to need 120 stones, laying them end to end, to make the walk."

"No," his beloved wife replied.

"What do you mean, no?"

"No. We're not putting them end to end. I want landscaping rock between the stepping stones," Cindy said.

Silence and bed space ensued—much wider than the parting of the Red Sea. This was a serious marital argument.

"Good night," they both said tersely.

More Red Sea silence. Then . . .

Wife of Moses: "I'm sorry I didn't communicate better with you on what I wanted for the walkway."

Moses: "It's silly to fight about rocks. That's why I didn't want to talk about this in bed."

Moses's wife: "At least we talked about it before you brought the garden center home." (Then wife, realizing irony, bursts into uncontrollable laughter. It is silly to be fighting over rocks.)

Moral: Sometimes you even have to fight about rocks.

Epilogue: Moses found some different, more holy rocks.

Wife agreed—with landscape stones between the rocks.
Walkway is beautiful; marriage is still intact.

And sealed with a kiss.

> The worst reconciliation is better
> than the best divorce.
>
> *Cervantes*

5
The Big S

Husbands are like fires. They go out when unattended.

Zsa Zsa Gabor

've never thought of Zsa Zsa as a great theologian, but she's right on the biblical mark there, intimacy-wise.

In Song of Songs, a beautiful Old Testament love poem between a newly married couple, it says, "Love is as strong as death. . . . It burns like blazing fire, like a mighty flame" (8:6). Later, in the New Testament, husbands and wives are cautioned not to deprive one another sexually. "The wife's body does not belong to her alone but also to her husband. In the same way, the husband's body does not belong to him alone but also to his wife. Do not deprive each other except by mutual consent and for a time, so that you may devote yourselves to prayer" (1 Cor. 7:4–5).

There goes the headache excuse, ladies.

Let's face it. Men are sex obsessed.

But prayer's a good one. What husband is going to object to "Not right now, dear. I'm praying"? Unless, of course, he wants to risk being branded a thoughtless, unspiritual, sex-obsessed animal.

And let's face it. Men *are* sex obsessed.

My writing pal Dave Meurer, who's been called the "Christian Dave Barry" and has been joyfully married for more than two decades to the wonderful, long-suffering Dale, wrote a hilarious marriage book a couple years ago called *Daze of Our Wives,* in which he devoted not one, not two, but THREE chapters to the subject of sex.

See, told you guys are sex obsessed.

Although Dave says that's an unfair stereotype.

Even as women are unfairly caricaturing us guys as having the sex drive of hyperactive weasels (For the record, the *Journal of the American Medical Association* has documented that men have the sex drive of hyperactive ferrets, not weasels. So there.) we men are quietly going about the daily business of paying our bills, getting the tires rotated, and engaging in a host of other productive activities, in many cases going an *entire five minutes* without thinking about sex, which proves that we are not obsessed with this topic, but merely very, very interested in it. (That's "very" to the twenty-fourth power.)

This high level of interest in sex is largely due to biological factors, and thus we guys could not change our colossal fascination with sex even if we wanted to, which we most certainly *don't*, because we really *like* being this way. It's fun! Just ask us! (If you happen to be married to us, that is!)

None of this is meant to imply that men *enjoy* sex more than women do. That is not at all the case. It's just that men *think* about sex so much more than women do, and men are also genetically designed to become amorous at a much lower threshold.[1]

Thanks for that male perspective, Dave. But we still think you guys are sex obsessed.

I wanted Michael's input here, but he's a very private guy—which he kind of had to give up once he married me, especially once I started writing books that laid bare nearly every facet of our lives—and was a little nervous when I told him about this chapter. "You're not going to write about our sex life for the whole world to read, are you?"

"Of course not, honey. I'm just going to write about everyone *else's* sex lives."

And so I am. Discreetly, of course. And within the bounds of good taste.

One of my girlfriends—I'll call her "Jill," since she too wanted to be discreet—said that when their marriage first began, she and her husband, "Frank," couldn't get enough of each other sexually. Then, over the years, as is common with many women, her sex drive decreased considerably.

"Now after we get the kids to sleep," Jill said, "the clock may say 9:54, and my husband wants to make love, so I'll say, 'Well, I want to be asleep by 10 p.m., so you've got six minutes.'"

But Jill isn't always such a sex Nazi. In fact, she's been known to turn the sex table on her husband occasionally.

To prevent pregnancy, she and Frank abstain from sex during her most fertile times, so after those abstinence days, she says he's excited and raring to go. One night, for a change, Jill took the sexual initiative.

"Aren't we going to make love?" she asked. "Let me go freshen up and I'll be right back."

As Jill headed to the bathroom, she overheard her husband say to himself in a gleeful whisper, "I'm gonna get lucky tonight."

After nearly fifteen years of marriage, this couple has learned how to best meet one another's needs in the bedroom.

"My 'foreplay' is my talking with his completely attentive ear—simply listening to me for twenty minutes," Jill said. "Then he'll say, 'Okay, have we had enough of your foreplay now?'"

She has also learned to use this time to share certain important, intimate things. "If I've charged something on a credit card, and I know I shouldn't have, I'll tell him during my foreplay time," she said. "That's the best time."

Another girlfriend says her best talking and sharing time with her husband is *after* sex. "Then he's a captive audience."

Works for me too. This is the one time when I have Michael's completely undivided attention and he doesn't mind talking about house plans, upcoming family events, our social calendar, or any other spur of the moment ideas I come up with.

"Rachel," another friend of mine, recently became an empty nester, as she and her husband, "Don," packed their last child off to college. With the kids gone, she says she and Don have showered more love and affection on their dog, Mugsy, whom they rescued from the pound—even allowing him to sleep in their bedroom now.

But there's a little problem.

"If Don and I even so much as hold hands—never mind

kiss—Mugsy puts his paws up on the edge of the bed and howls!" she said.

Now when one of them gets unexpectedly romantic, they have to catch the dog, drag him out from behind the furniture, and take him outside, then come in and wash the doggy smell off their hands.

Michael and I don't have that problem. Maybe that's because we have a girl dog.

Gracie's such a little lady that when we start to get a little amorous, she gives us an embarrassed, slightly jealous look over her shoulder—we had her "fixed" years ago—and promptly trots out of the room.

I want to close this chapter with a couple more paragraphs from my friend Dave's wonderful and hilarious—yet also occasionally deep and spiritual—book.

> I think God uses our sexual desire to move us toward commitment, trust, sacrifice, wrenching honesty, and all kinds of stuff you experience in marriage—stuff many males would probably avoid like Tupperware parties were it not for this potent, marvelous craving we call sex.
>
> God uses sex to lull us into those other things we really need—emotional connectedness, selflessness, loyalty, and excellent cardiovascular exercise.[2]

Gotta run. I'm feeling the need for a little emotional connectedness with my husband right now.

One of my theories is that men love with their
eyes; women love with their ears.

Zsa Zsa Gabor

6

Dollar Dilemmas

I believe that love cannot be bought except with love,

and he who has a good wife wears heaven in his hat.

John Steinbeck

'm not good with money.

Ask my husband. But it's not my fault. I'd be okay if numbers weren't involved.

Before we got married, I was of the monetary mind-set that to balance my checkbook meant to call the bank—this was before Internet banking—and find out my balance. That was how much I had left to spend.

The concept of outstanding checks was completely foreign. I guess maybe I thought those were the really good ones.

Although Michael is no Larry Burkett or Louis Rukeyser—the guy on *Wall Street Week*—he is better than I am with finances. (My sweetie wanted to add that this is not saying much.) So after the wedding, he took care of the fiscal matters.

> *The concept of outstanding checks was completely foreign. I guess maybe I thought those were the really good ones.*

A few years later, I got frustrated one evening. I didn't have one *clue* as to what we paid to whom or how much we owed on what. After I'd vented my frustration, Michael agreed that I should know what was going on with our finances and said he would take care of it. He began keeping a log sheet with all the account information.

Knowing that this financial information was all there at my fingertips, I promptly forgot all about it. He had it under control, after all.

Two and a half years later I got frustrated one evening.

I didn't have one clue as to what we paid or how much we owed on what. After I'd vented my frustration, Michael calmly walked into his office and pulled out a ledger. The one that sits with the bills yet to be paid in it. And he showed me the log sheet. There was everything listed by account and month.

For the entire year.

And last year.

And the year before that.

That's when we both realized I hadn't looked at the ledger since he'd started it two and a half years before. But it was nice to actually see that he had it all so organized and under control.

I have numbers vertigo.

As I glanced at the page, all those numbers started swimming around. It was like I was in a movie. Yeah, that Hitchcock movie with Jimmy Stewart and Kim Novak. And I was Jimmy looking down from the tower into the psychedelic swirling.

That's it. I have numbers vertigo. It has a name.

So what was I thinking when I insisted on paying the bills?

About four or five years ago, we were having one of those marital discussions about money.

You know those discussions. The ones that often end with one person saying, "Fine," the other one saying, "Fine!" and then one or both repeating, "FINE!" and sometimes slamming a door.

Michael was going through a particularly stressful period at work and was overwhelmed with that and all the at-home responsibilities as well. So being the good, loving wife that I am, I offered to help ease his stress.

I said *I* would pay the bills.

Since he was keeping such a great ledger, it would be easy to continue his system. Even I could handle it. Piece of cake. Wedding cake with six layers of different fillings.

Compared to my past history, I did a bang-up job paying the bills. Until Michael opened the mail one day to see that our car insurance had been canceled. He called our insurance agent, who reminded him of their rule stating that if we're late paying our premium two months in a row, the policy is automatically canceled.

We had another one of those marital discussions.

Yes, I'd paid all the bills. Usually on time. Most of the time. When it's due on the fifteenth and I mail it that day, why would they consider that late?

Michael offered to take back the responsibility for paying the bills. And he's been paying them ever since.

Works for me.

One thing most people don't realize is that, in general, authors only get "paychecks" three or four times a year—depending on how many new projects they're working on at the time or drumming up for the future.

a kiss is still a kiss

Once, when we received a slightly larger than expected royalty check from the sales of two of my books, I wanted to take that "extra" money to pay off a big bill so we could cross it off our list. (Don't you just love crossing off bills from your debt list? I do. Feels great!)

But my wise, practical husband intervened. "No, honey. We need to put that money in savings to stretch out over all those months when you *don't* get a paycheck."

Spoilsport.

I was just trying to help us get out of debt. If we kept putting money in savings, I didn't see how that would ever happen. I mean, who needs groceries?

A few years ago, Michael and I agreed on a clever financial plan that has worked out quite well for us: we both receive an "allowance" every two weeks when Michael gets paid. (Something my friend Katie suggested that has worked very well in her marriage. Thanks, Katie!)

I hadn't gotten an allowance since I was a kid.

And at first I wasn't sure how I was going to like this. After all, I'm a grown-up and responsible. Why couldn't I just use our money when I wanted for what I wanted?

At least part of that middle statement was true. The grown-up part.

Katie's allowance idea was the best thing for the dueling dollars dilemma we faced in our marriage.

Every two weeks on Michael's payday, we each get the same amount of money to do whatever we want with—no questions asked. Michael has "his" money, and I have "mine." If I want to go to lunch or the movies with a girlfriend, that comes out of my allowance. Or if I want to buy a book or CD I've been coveting—also out of my allowance. (Forget buying thick, brand-new hardbacks though—that would eat up most of my allotment.)

We can also use our allowance to treat the other one to a surprise lunch or dinner or to buy a little gift for the other if we so choose.

Or if you're Michael, you can set some money aside to save up for a big-ticket item you really want. Like a weekend trip to Disneyland.

Michael has an old college friend who works down at Disneyland whom he likes to go visit occasionally. But at this particular time, we'd agreed to use all our extra income toward bills—no vacations or clothes or any of that fun, frivolous, and nonessential stuff. And I didn't see any room in our budget for a trip to Disneyland—even though Michael wouldn't have to pay for lodging and his friend could get him into the park for free.

So my smart and frugal husband decided he'd save for Disneyland out of his allowance. After all, that was "his" money to do whatever he wanted with, no questions asked.

Worked for me, although I couldn't imagine how my darling would be able to save up for a trip on such meager fare.

But he did. He stopped buying sodas at work, and where before he'd taken a sack lunch three or four days and eaten out maybe once or twice a week with co-workers, now he brown-bagged it every day.

Michael decided to set aside half of his allowance for our upcoming trip to England as well. And I decided to join him in this great idea. But by the time we boarded our flight for the UK, Michael had saved over two hundred dollars. I'd saved twenty dollars.

There went my pretty teapot. Told you I wasn't good with money.

Although I'm starting to get a little better, thanks to an eye-opening incident a few months ago. There was a brand-new movie opening on a Friday night that I really wanted to see, so I decided to treat myself to a nice sit-down dinner and movie with my niece Kari. (Usually, to save money, we go to matinees and either eat lunch at home or do a cheap drive-through.)

But I felt like a fun girls' night. And it *was* fun. We had a great time.

Until I looked in my wallet at the end of the evening and noticed the four paltry dollars there—all that remained of my two-week allowance.

Now if I do a night movie, I don't go out to dinner too (unless Michael pays). Matinees rule.

More than forty years ago, my aunt Sharon and uncle Jim were saving for a down payment on a house, using monthly savings bonds mailed to them by Jim's work. One month, Jim asked Sharon if the savings bond had arrived yet, and she said she hadn't seen it.

So Jim called in to work to check, and of course, the bond had been mailed.

Then Sharon remembered. Just that morning, she'd decided to go through all the junk mail that had been accumulating and throw it out. Could she possibly have thrown it out by mistake? She had. And it took sifting through lots of yucky, disgusting garbage to find that out.

"Of course, for months and years after that, Jim said to me, 'So did you throw anything away today?'"

Christie said her husband, Greg, recently approached her with the dreaded task of reorganizing their financial files.

"When I was young, filing was the only part of working at the library I didn't enjoy," she recalled. "I figured we could take a shortcut by just filing our old check registers in the horror genre and be done with it.

"But afterward, it was easier for us to track in what areas we had overspent," Christie said. "This was a useful exercise, because we did pin down that even though it is nice of me to want to buy clothes for our kids when I notice their wardrobes lacking—I was feeling like a very valuable Proverbs 31 woman when my husband started out by mentioning this—I should *wash* their clothes instead of running out and buying them some more.

"So much for being a Proverbs 31 woman."

Michael and I are big *Jeopardy* fans. It's the only TV show we watch every night, and we have lots of fun playing along with the contestants. I'm pretty fast on the uptake and always do well, so I have this fantasy of appearing on the show someday and winning lots of money.

Only problem is, I guess the answers correctly and amass a large sum by the end of the show, but even when I get the final jeopardy question right, I lose to the other contestants because I never wager properly. That involves math and numbers, and I mess up every time.

Maybe I should try out for *Who Wants to Be a Millionaire?* instead, where they just give you the money when you get the answers correct.

Although, since I can never get through on their phone lines, I think I might have a better chance praying for a best seller instead. You can help me in this quest. Please join me in prayer, then go buy several copies of this book and give them to friends as gifts.

My husband, my publisher, and my bank account will thank you.

It is better to have a rich soul than to be rich.

Olga Korbut

7

The In-Law Files

A sound marriage is not based on complete frankness;

it is based on a sensible reticence.

Morris L. Ernst

"Why is your mother that way?"

"Well, why's your brother that way?"

Welcome to the world of in-laws. Someone once said that when you marry a person, you're not marrying just that person, you're marrying his or her family too.

Give that person a cigar. Or better yet, a stick of sugar-free gum.

In-laws can make life interesting.

If you're fortunate, like me, you'll acquire a set of in-laws you like—make that *love*—and get along with. But even when you like and love them, there can be little in-law idiosyncrasies you need to adjust to.

> *Even when you like and love them, there can be little in-law idiosyncrasies you need to adjust to.*

Take Bill and Susie, who've been married a couple decades. Early in their marriage, the young couple had just bought their first house, and before they moved in, they gave Susie's parents a key to meet some workmen who would be arriving when they were both at work.

"My parents never did give the key back," Susie recalled, "even though we mentioned it several times. It was always 'in my other purse,' 'at home,' or 'we may need it again someday.'"

The couple would come home from work and find notes from Susie's mother on the counter, or she'd be waiting for them in their living room.

"She never knocked and would just let herself in even when we were home," Susie said. "Finally Bill decided he'd had enough. One evening while I was still at work, he heard her car drive up, and he took off all his clothes except his underwear and met her at the door as she let herself in."

Bill loudly announced to his mother-in-law that he and his wife were having sex in the kitchen, then shut the door and locked it.

His mother-in-law drove away. But she still never gave the key back.

"She started letting herself in again about six months later and has never stopped," Susie said. "But now she always rings the bell first and waits a little while—in case we're home."

Angela, a friend of a friend, had a different in-law embarrassment early in her marriage.

She and her new husband, on the way home from their romantic honeymoon getaway, spent the last night of the honeymoon with his parents. They were sound asleep—really —when in the middle of the night, the bed broke, dumping them on the floor.

Angela had a hard time facing her in-laws the next morning.

Dan from Illinois, who's been married to his wife, Ann, for eighteen years, shared this delightful in-laws story with me.

"My wife is her parents' only girl and was the first of her

 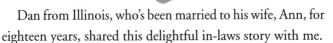

siblings to get married," Dan related. "We married young—I was twenty-one and Ann was nineteen when we packed all our belongings in a six-by-nine U-Haul and moved to my first Air Force duty assignment in upstate New York."

The newlyweds looked for a house to rent but, unable to find one that fit their needs, wound up buying a small three-bedroom ranch house in Verona, New York.

"On the first spring visit, my in-laws—who have lived on a farm all their life—decided that we needed a garden plot," Dan said. "After all, we were on a tight budget with the home purchase, and we had both grown up with gardens at home."

However, there wasn't much space on their new property for a garden. Just across the street, though, there was an empty lot that was overgrown waist high with dead grass and brush.

"One afternoon while I was at work and the ladies were working in the house, my father-in-law grabbed a shovel and started working on creating a garden plot on the empty lot," Dan recalled. "It was difficult to deal with the overgrowth, so he tackled it just like he would back on the farm. He got some gasoline and matches and proceeded to burn the brush off of the empty lot."

That day Dan received a phone call at work saying that the town of Verona police and fire departments were both at his house. They'd been called by a neighbor who saw the rip-roaring blaze in the empty lot.

"After the fire was extinguished and the fire department left, I explained to the elderly lady who lived next door to, and owned, the empty lot that my father-in-law was well meaning and didn't think anyone owned the lot. She was fine with the idea of having a garden plot on the vacant lot. She just wished someone would have asked her first.

"Thankfully, she didn't press any charges," Dan said.

"In the long run, my father-in-law's backcountry ways resulted in a good-town neighbor relationship the entire time we lived in that home. Our neighbor frequently stopped by to chat while we worked in the garden, and we frequently stopped by her house with fresh produce."

My Texas friend Annette's father gave her and her husband, Randy—along with any other young people who were about to be married—a great piece of newlywed advice: "Move away from both sets of parents so you can begin married life on your own."

Annette and Randy took her dad's advice to heart and moved away from their small Texas town, across three states and two major rivers to Colorado, a week after their wedding. They packed up all their possessions in the smallest U-Haul that could be rented and drove off into the sunset.

"We said a big, teary good-bye to his folks, then got to the edge of town and had car trouble. We had to call his dad to come get us," Annette said. "It was terribly embarrassing."

Although Randy and Annette didn't stay in Colorado long—they've lived in Texas most of their twenty-five years of married life—rarely have they lived in the same town as either set of parents. Usually, they're at least an hour's drive away.

They love their folks dearly but took Annette's daddy's counsel to heart and as a result have enjoyed a good relationship with both sets of in-laws over the years.

The same holds true for my longtime friends Pat and Ken, who've been married more than thirty-five years. They met and married in college, and shortly afterward, Ken joined the Air Force and had to report to officer training school (OTS) in San Antonio, Texas. For the next fifteen years, Pat was an Air Force wife, living all over the globe—from Florida to Las Vegas to Southern California to England. Other than a brief period when Pat lived back home while Ken was stationed in Thailand, the couple has never lived in the same town as either of their families.

Bob and Debbie, on the other hand, had both sets of family nearby, which made it difficult, especially at the holidays.

"When we first got married, he didn't want to ever go to my family's for any function whatsoever," Debbie recalled. "So

a kiss is still a kiss

over time, I would just go without him. Eventually, when he realized I attended functions with his family—and enjoyed most of them—he started to come around and go to mine. Now we try to compromise: one Christmas with my family, one Christmas Eve with his."

Sheri, Michael's sister, had a bit of a rude awakening when she married into her husband, Jim's, family.

"Married women didn't get to sit at the table with the big folks to eat," Sheri said. "Young women of childbearing age had to sit at the kids' table. Plus, women didn't get toothpicks in the Jameson family. They were reserved for men only because it wasn't ladylike for a woman to pick her teeth."

When Sheri was dating Jim, she got to sit at the big table, but once they were married and she was pregnant, she had to sit in the kitchen with the kids.

My no-nonsense sister-in-law staged a sit-in a couple times in a rocker in the living room, and her husband stuck up for her.

Jim told his family, "If Sheri can't sit here at the table with me, I'm not going to sit here either."

That broke the tradition.

Some traditions have their roots in strong ethnic backgrounds.

Once upon a time, a nice Anglo girl named Jeanette married a nice Mexican boy named Ricardo, and they lived bliss-fully together as bride and groom in the great state of Texas. At the first outdoor gathering of Ricardo's large family—he had eight siblings—when the buffet-style dinner was ready, all the women lined up first while the men remained sitting down.

Newlywed Jeanette followed suit, filled her plate, sat down, and began to eat. Then she looked around and noticed she was the only woman eating. The other wives hadn't been fix-ing their own plates when they went through the buffet line; they'd each filled their husbands' plates and served them, as good Latin wives were wont to do.

Then there's my Chinese friend Rebecca. Her mother-in-law is older and very traditional, coming from an old-world, orthodox, and conventional Chinese background.

"She really wanted grandchildren," Rebecca recalled, "and tried so hard not to pressure us. But she'd come up to me and put her hand on me and say, 'How are you?' and I knew just what she was implying."

But my friend understood. And didn't mind. Besides, she said she's home free now.

"Having twin boys is hitting the jackpot," Rebecca said. "I'm off the hook as a daughter-in-law now. No matter what, I *did* produce them, so I'm not a bad wife."

Annette's mother, like her dad, also imparted a little marital wisdom to her children—but she demonstrated hers with action rather than advice.

"My mom really courted all of her in-law children," my girlfriend said. "She was determined that they were going to like her."

For instance, growing up, Annette and her siblings never had sodas in the house—no Cokes, not even any of that sweet Texas nectar, Dr Pepper. Her parents never bought them. So my friend was thoroughly miffed when after her brother married Martha, her mom kept a supply of Pepsi in the house for her new daughter-in-law.

Annette's husband also benefited from his mother-in-law's graciousness.

"Randy's not an adventurous eater," Annette confided. "So for about five years running, every time we went to my mom and dad's house for dinner, she fixed the same thing, Randy's favorite meal: hamburger steak, mashed potatoes, and cherry pie.

"I got so sick of the same thing every time," my Southern-fried friend said. "She never fixed *my* favorite meal."

I asked Annette what her favorite meal was. "Well, I'm a little weird," my vegetable-loving friend replied. "If it's slimy and green, I like it."

"What about chicken?" I asked. "Do you like chicken?"

"We'd never have chicken at my house. Dad's a cattle rancher."

"Huh?"

"My mom doesn't cook chicken 'cause my dad considers it an insult," Annette explained. "It's kind of like if your dad has a Ford lot, you don't drive a Chevy."

Oh.

My mom has always done nice things for her children-in-law as well.

When Michael and I first got married, he reacted badly to sugar, which made it difficult around the holidays—especially Christmas, with all the yummy cookies and candy everyone was scarfing down. Mom always made a point of driving to a bakery across town that specialized in sugar-free goodies to buy Michael some special treats for the holiday.

My mom adores my husband and is always doing sweet, thoughtful things for him. Recently, he had hernia surgery, and while he was recuperating, she brought him a get-well gift that he loved: a ship's wheel clock. (Michael loves anything to do with the sea, so his entire arts and crafts studio is decorated with all things nautical.)

And he's returned the favor by making her some beautiful quilts and tablecloths.

Sheri had this in-law story to share: "Do not fly in to visit your husband's sister and brother-in-law if there's a pro ball game going on—they'll leave you sitting at the airport until it's finished."

One trip when Sheri called her brother-in-law's house to let them know her plane had landed, one of the guys picked up the phone and said, "We'll be there as soon as the game's over."

When exactly *was* that, my sister-in-law wondered.

She found out three hours later when they finally arrived to pick her up.

> For this reason a man will leave his father
> and mother and be united to his wife,
> and they will become one flesh.
>
> *Genesis 2:24*

8
Art Appreciation 101

Art is like a border of flowers along the course of civilization.

Lincoln Steffens

M ichael is a culture vulture.

This drew us together in our dating days, since I'd much rather go to the movies, the theater, a gallery opening, or ANYthing to do with the arts than anything related to sports. And in my beloved, I found a kindred artistic spirit.

He was delighted to discover the same in me.

Or so he thought.

Then he had another one of those rude Jekyll/Hyde awakenings when we went to the ballet for the first time as a couple to see a production of *Romeo and Juliet*.

Unlike most men, Michael loves the ballet.

The grace, the beauty, the elegant way the prima ballerina extends her delicate hand, the high leaps, the twirls, the tutus. His interest in ballet is a natural extension of his love of watching and performing in musical theater. When Michael worked for a professional theater company years ago, their choreographer was a soloist with the Houston Ballet, so he had the privilege of knowing several of the dancers on a personal basis. And naturally, he saw lots of ballets.

But his favorites are the classics, and he was excited to share that wonderful cultural experience with me.

As the curtain fell after Romeo and Juliet's tragic death scene, Michael turned to me with shining eyes and said, "Well, did you like it?"

"It was nice," I admitted. "But I'd have liked it better if there had been words."

What can I say?

I make my living with words, and they're my preferred art form. Although I admired the grace and beauty of the dancers, after two hours of leaping and twirling and grand jetéing about, I was a little bored.

a kiss is still a kiss

At least I didn't fall asleep.

Which is what happened the first time I went to the opera. In my early twenties. In London—a gorgeous production of *La Bohème*. This time there were words. But they were in Italian. And other than *scusi, prego,* and Luciano Pavarotti, I didn't know any Italian. And the theater was a little warm, so by the end of the second act, I was sound asleep.

I'm happy to report, however, that I've never fallen asleep in an art museum.

When my darling and I were dating, I described my visits to the Louvre in Paris and my first heart-stopping view of the Venus de Milo and Winged Victory, all the Rembrandts at the Rijksmuseum in Amsterdam, Degas' ballet dancers in Edinburgh, and countless trips to London's amazing National Gallery with its Impressionism bounty.

> *I do love art. Just not to the same degree or intensity that my husband does. I possess more of a fast-food drive-through McArt mentality. "I'll take a Renoir and a side of Monet to go— but please hold the Andy Warhol."*

Michael was enraptured and more than a little envious. Naturally, he thought I was an art lover too. Particularly because my beloved father was an artist and I grew up around his painting.

I do love art. Just not to the same degree or intensity that my husband does. I possess more of a fast-food drive-through McArt mentality. "I'll take a Renoir and a side of Monet to go—but please hold the Andy Warhol."

Which Michael discovered much to his dismay the first time we visited a well-known art museum in San Francisco. We had walked through most of the museum in an hour or so when Michael noticed that a tour was about to begin. Of course, he wanted to take it.

I didn't understand why. To me, we'd already seen the museum—it would be a waste of time to go back and see the same paintings again. But to Michael, our walk-through was just an orientation. Now that he knew the lay of the museum, he was ready to dig in and really *see* the paintings.

But I was tired and hungry, and Ghiradelli Square was calling my name. That time my base nature won out over Michael's more artistic one.

Years later when we visited New York City during a book tour—Michael's first time in the Big Apple—he spent eight hours at the Metropolitan Museum of Art while I was doing publicity and media interviews. That night he told me he'd spent five hours in nineteenth-century Europe alone and had only three hours left to see the other twenty-something centuries.

Our last day in the city, he was itching to go back to the Met and take *me* to see this most amazing place.

Philistine that I am, I zipped in and out in about forty-five minutes.

Poor Michael. At least I don't belch and scratch and watch football.

Well, two out of three isn't bad.

One of my husband's favorite art museums in the world is the Art Institute of Chicago, with its gorgeous, grand stone lions at the entrance. He first discovered it on a trip with his sister, Sheri—they spent six hours there and only scratched the surface. But Michael says it's where he learned how to "do a museum."

Sheri and Michael each bought a companion guidebook and started in the basement, working their way up to the Impressionists. When they came upon a piece of art shown in the guidebook, they'd stop and read about it. But there was still more museum than hours to see it. That trip, Michael learned that there was just too much to see in one day, so he learned to focus on one area or period—like the nineteenth century.

My sweet, art-lovin' guy loves to get the audio guide offered at many museums—a personal CD player with headphones. Many of the paintings have numbers. No, not paint by number. The painting descriptions are listed numerically on the guide, and you press a specific number and hear about a specific painting. Though he never studied French, Michael can now properly pronounce Argenteuil and Giverny—thanks to the audio guide.

On another trip to Chicago, Michael, my mom, and I spent about an hour together in the Art Institute before stopping for lunch. Afterward, Mom and I headed to the gift shop, while Michael went back into the museum.

It is, after all, one of his favorites.

The hook that brought Michael to Chicago in the first place was George Seurat's *Sunday Afternoon on the Island of Grand Jatte.* That painting and its artist were the inspiration of the Broadway musical *Sunday in the Park with George,* starring Mandy Patinkin. Since that's one of Michael's favorite shows, he jumped at the chance to visit Chicago to see the painting.

And he wasn't disappointed.

Funny how appreciation for one art form often leads to an exploration of other art forms. Take movies—my other favorite medium. Movies are a great way to learn about new art forms.

When I saw *Camille Claudel*—the story of the woman sculptor who was in love with and posed for Rodin, starring the amazing Isabelle Adjani and Gérard Depardieu—it gave me a new appreciation for sculpture as an art form.

a kiss is still a kiss

I was first drawn to sculpture's beauty at the Louvre when I saw the Winged Victory those many years ago, but now, as a result of seeing this movie and knowing this fascinating story, sculpture means so much more to me.

As does opera. Thanks to Michael and the Academy Award–winning movie *Moonstruck*.

In this delightful original movie that has that great line of Cher's, "Snap out of it!" Nicolas Cage takes Cher to the Metropolitan Opera for her very first time to see *La Bohème*. There's a gorgeous scene where the doomed lovers are singing, and we see a close-up of Cher weeping from the sheer beauty of the music.

So how come I fell asleep at that same *La Bohème* years earlier?

Perhaps because I was young. Or because I didn't know enough. Or because they didn't have subtitles. (Yes, they have subtitles at the opera now, so you know what the characters are saying.) Whatever the reason, I recently told Michael I'd like to see *La Bohème* again. With him. Since our marriage, I've fallen in love with Puccini and have even taken to listening to it in the mornings.

When Michael and I traveled to London on vacation in the spring of 2003, my husband thought he'd died and gone to culture vulture heaven. Seven days wasn't nearly enough time for him to see everything he wanted to see.

But after four days in this exciting, cosmopolitan capital, I was chomping at the bit to get out of the big city and return to the tranquil countryside. Where I could read and have a nice cuppa tea.

That's when my beloved and I realized we had some serious Jekyll/Hyde travel differences.

At least by now we'd learned that our art appreciation was at different levels, so when we visited the world-famous National Gallery, where I'd gone more than a dozen times when I was stationed in England years earlier, we split up. Michael went on a four-hour guided tour, where they spent fifteen minutes learning about a specific painting.

Since I can't imagine spending fifteen minutes talking about ONE painting, I did the quick zip-and-trip method, perfect for Philistines with short attention spans.

A while back, my Texas friend Annette hosted her aunt and uncle and their Scottish friends John and Pauline (all in their sixties—except Annette) for lunch. During their conversation, Annette mentioned that her high school daughter Rachel had been to the ballet the night before with her class.

Pauline then launched into a fun story—in her wonderful Scottish accent—about her hubby: "John rather likes modern ballet, but classical is not to his taste," she said. "Even so, he's good about going with me. Whenever we go, I must make sure he has an aisle seat though. He does fairly well in the beginning scenes when the lovely girls come out in their tutus—I think he rather enjoys that part. But then when the men come out in their tights, I feel him begin to take lots of deep breaths. Then he starts to tremble and shake." (Here Pauline demonstrated something rather like controlled convulsions to Annette.)

"Then I hear him make this awful noise—like a closed-mouth cross between a howl and a snort," Pauline said. "Soon John bolts from his seat and dashes to the lobby of the hall. Everyone around us assumes John is having a heart attack and that I must be very cold to sit there, oblivious, enjoying the show."

Sheri and Jim had a similar experience when she took him to see the *Nutcracker*—the first time he'd ever gone to the ballet. "He started laughing out loud," Sheri recalled, "and all these old ladies were shushing him."

Public art is one thing. But how do you handle private art?

My girlfriend Rebecca wants to know how to reconcile different artistic tastes in the marital household. For instance, her husband, Waymond, loves avant-garde modern art.

Way avant-garde.

Rebecca likes modern art too, just not some of the way out stuff her husband enjoys.

"When you get married, how do you decide?" Rebecca asked. "Usually, women have control over the house, but in all fairness, if you have a husband and he wants to hang some art he really likes, you should let him do it."

Rebecca stuck to her loving, equitable decorating guns until the day Waymond came home with an "appalling but very valuable photograph" of something that wasn't at all an enjoyable thing to look at. (We won't discuss what it was.)

"He spent his own money, and it was something that meant a lot to him, but it wasn't something I felt comfortable hanging in our house for everyone to see," my friend said. "How do you compromise on something like that? How much of his taste is he allowed to hang up in the house? And how to say it without hurting his feelings?"

It's called the garage.

Rebecca, like countless married women before her, finally realized the wifely wisdom of men getting designated areas in the house.

Or attached to the house.

"I used to wonder, *Why are all these guys out in the garage?—Steve Jobs, Bill Hewlett, Dave Packard . . .* It's because their wives say, 'Take that stuff out of here,'" Rebecca surmised.

a kiss is still a kiss

"That's why so many great inventions in the twentieth century were in the garage."

So that old saying is true after all: "Behind every successful man is a great woman."

In *Dated Jekyll, Married Hyde*, I devoted a whole chapter to that conundrum, called "His Junk, My Treasures." While researching that chapter, I realized I didn't have it so bad when Michael and I got married, since some of Michael's favorite artistic things at the time were plastic Disney figures of Mickey Mouse and his pals.

At least he didn't insist on hanging a velvet Elvis in our living room flanked by an ancient wasp's nest.

Yes, a wasp's nest.

My friend Michelle's husband, Doug, had discovered the nest when he was a boy and patiently spent hours unearthing it from the dirt. All his hard work paid off, because when he finally pulled it out, it was completely intact.

He was so proud of his archaeological find that he hung it in his bedroom, where it stayed for years. When he moved out, he took his beloved nest with him—much to his mother's delight. All through college, it hung in his living room.

And when Michelle married him, it was a case of "Love me, love my nest."

Although she never quite grew to love his childhood treasure, she did tolerate it.

Until they moved. Then she was able to banish the nest to the spare room.

As for Elvis, Doug wasn't even a fan. He just loved the wonderful tackiness of the king on black velvet.

Elvis started in the living room, graduated to the dining room, and finally wound up in the garage. But recently Michelle was happy to report that "Elvis has now left the building."[3]

Every child is an artist. The problem is how to remain an artist once he grows up.

Pablo Picasso

a kiss is still a kiss

9

And Then They Had Kids

What feeling is so nice as a child's hand in yours? So small, so soft and warm, like a kitten huddling in the shelter of your clasp.

Marjorie Holmes

Michael and I don't have children—at least of the two-footed variety. But we're the proud parents of Princess Grace Elizabeth, an American Eskimo dog.

And Gracie sure has made a difference in our marital life.

She's the greatest argument stopper ever invented. Gracie doesn't like it when we have a discussion that involves raised voices or angry tones. Her little ears—which usually stand up all happy and perky—go straight back, and she comes and paws at us, climbing up our chests and gently thumping us with her creamy white paws to say in her own little way, "Stop yelling!"

We think every married couple needs a Gracie in their life.

Even if she's of the two-legged variety.

Our friends Chris and Steve, who've been married fourteen years, have five children—the youngest named Gracie.

Yep. You heard me. Five.

And these five children are all nine years old and under.

"Whenever we go out places, people are constantly asking, 'Are they all yours?'" Chris said.

Recently, when Chris and I were talking on the phone after being out of touch for a couple years, I heard baby Gracie fussing in the background. As a way of making polite kid conversation, I asked Chris, "So are you going to be having any more?" fully expecting the answer to be a loud, emphatic no.

But Chris surprised me when she said yes.

"When you get past three [children], it really doesn't matter," she said matter-of-factly. "You might as well keep on going."

Chris and Steve have their child rearing down to a loving science. They live in a rambling, two-story house in the gorgeous foothills outside of Sacramento, where Chris homeschools the kids while Steve runs their candle business.

She loves her stay-at-home profession. "I have the best job in the whole world," Chris said.

When she goes out to run errands or go shopping with all the kids in tow, she's purposeful and intently focused on what she's doing, not having time for idle chitchat. She wants to get in the store, buy what she needs, and get out. So that's what's on her mind. And she's oblivious to the stares of other shoppers around her.

When you get past three [children], it really doesn't matter. You might as well keep on going.

Until Daniel, her seven-year-old and only boy, whispers, "Mom, I think people are *counting* us . . ."

"People will come up to me and say, 'We've been watching you and can't believe you have five kids and they're so well behaved,'" Chris told me.

I feel the same way.

I recently visited Chris and Steve and their family at their great home with a view, after not having been there in about four or five years, and was simply amazed. The children—all nine and under, mind you—were polite, well mannered, and simply delightful.

"We try to be consistent with their discipline without anger," Chris said, "although we're still learning that. If I do get angry with them and raise my voice, they say—with all respect, of course—'Now, Mommy, remember, a gentle answer turns away wrath, but a harsh word stirs up anger.' They often quote Proverbs to me."

My friend is the first to admit that things aren't always picture-perfect in their well-run household—they're human, after all—acknowledging that she tends to get irritable at times. "They know not to mess with Mommy," Chris said, "because Mommy's in charge, and it could get ugly."

Her irritation extends to her husband, Steve, on occasion too.

That's when Hannah, the eldest child and the pragmatic peacemaker of the bunch, will say, "Okay, Mommy. Daddy said he's sorry. Now can we watch the movie?"

Hannah paved the way for the other kids. Since she was the firstborn, Steve and Chris, like many new parents, wanted to do everything by the book, so they were a bit more restrictive with her upbringing. But after the other kids started coming one right after another, they relaxed and eased up.

"Now we don't sweat the small stuff," Chris said.

Occasionally, the couple will go out on a double date with friends who have older kids. "That way, their kids watch ours," Chris said. "When you go out in public with the family, you're like a sergeant always reminding them of all the rules, so it's nice to have a break and be with grown-ups sometimes."

A few years ago, when the couple had just three kids, Chris made plans for a romantic weekend getaway to Santa Cruz—just the two of them. "All we did was talk about the kids," she recalled with a smile. "We were lovesick for our little family."

They haven't booked any romantic getaways à deux since, preferring instead to enjoy their romance at home when the kids have gone to sleep.

The happy couple has established a routine that works well for them. In the mornings, they get up at 5:30, work out, have their Bible study, and take a shower. After breakfast, when Steve leaves for work, they'll say to each other, "Bye, Mom. Bye, Dad."

"But on Friday night he's Big Daddy," Chris said.

Hannah, a wonderful student with excellent grades, is also the "gadget girl" in the family. "Once when we were shopping, she found one of those plastic clothes sensors lying on the floor," Chris recalled, "so she picked it up and put it in her pocket."

Unfortunately, when the family went to leave, all the store

alarms went off and security personnel had to check Chris's bags. "We couldn't figure out what the problem was," she said. "The beeping just kept going on and on. Finally, one of the store clerks said, 'Maybe the little girl has a sensor in her pocket?'"

Sure enough, a very red-faced Hannah did.

"She was so embarrassed, because she doesn't like to be the center of attention," Chris said. "At least I don't ever have to worry about them stealing something."

Although little Mary Elisabeth has been a little sticky-fingered at home now and then.

Chris keeps a candy stash in the pantry, and the kids must always ask for permission before getting a piece. One day, all on her own, Mary Elisabeth came up to Chris to confess. "I'm really sorry, Mommy," she said. "I'm sorry that I steal candy from the pantry. I take it without telling you, and I *always* do it. I sin and I don't mean to, and I don't want to go to hell."

Mary Elisabeth is the dramatic one in the family. And also the most vocal.

When she was four, her youngest sister, Gracie, was just a few months old, and Chris was breast-feeding. One Sunday morning at church, Chris had stepped out of the sanctuary for just a few moments, leaving Steve with the kids, when all of a sudden, Gracie began to cry.

Loudly.

Little Mary Elisabeth turned to the woman seated in the pew next to her—whom she didn't know—and said, "Gracie's crying because she wants to chew on Mommy's breast."

Later the woman approached Chris with a smile. "Your daughter explained to me why your infant was crying." A red-faced Chris later explained to Mary Elisabeth how it wasn't polite to talk to other people about Mommy's breasts.

Mary Elisabeth is the one who also liked to nurse her dolly. "She'd lift up her shirt, put the dolly to her chest, and hold her there for a while," Chris said. When her parents would tell her to put her shirt back down, Mary Elisabeth would say, "She's not finished yet." Afterward, she'd always burp the baby.

Her dolly, I mean.

Abigail, Chris and Steve's three-year-old, is much more shy, less talkative, and still very clingy with Mommy. Recently she had to see the doctor for an ear infection.

"She won't let anyone touch her, and I knew in advance that she was going to scream bloody murder," Chris recalled, "so I gently explained to her that they don't want to hurt her; they just want to help her. Then I gave her a blow-by-blow account of what to expect at the doctor's office: we'll get weighed and get our temperature taken, and the doctor will look in your ears."

Abigail still screamed once she got to the doctor's office.

Then Chris instructed her daughter, "Now, Abigail, you need to step on the scale," but Abigail wasn't having any of that either.

So the nurse told Chris to step on the scale too.

"Pardon?" my friend said.

Chris didn't scream, but she sure wasn't a happy camper.

Mother and daughter were weighed together. Then Mom had to be weighed separately, and her weight was subtracted from the total to give the nurse Abigail's weight.

As Chris drove her now content-to-be-just-with-Mom daughter home, she said lovingly, "Hey, Abs, thanks for broadcasting *my* weight at your doctor's appointment, honey."

Daniel, their second eldest, is the only boy in the family and has been longing for a brother for quite a while. "When we found out I was pregnant with Gracie, Daniel broke down and cried," Chris recalled. "He said, 'No, we've been praying for *Joel*!'"

But he loves his baby sister Gracie, and besides, his prayer may soon come true, as Chris and Steve would like to have one more child.

Unfortunately, others don't get pregnant quite so easily.

Our friends Rebecca and Waymond married a little later in life—having both done the coveted power careers and having

a kiss is still a kiss

lived the glamorous San Francisco Bay area lifestyle, only to realize how ultimately unfulfilling it was.

"Thank God we found each other in the nick of time," Rebecca said.

They went into their marriage right away trying to have children. "That's one of the many reasons we decided to move to a bucolic part of Sacramento, where Waymond had grown up and his parents still lived," my friend said.

The couple was busy building their dream house, so they didn't worry much about pregnancy during construction, thinking it was a blessing in disguise that nothing was happening on the biological front at that time. But then the house was all done, designed specifically with a big family in mind, and the couple sensed there might be a problem.

One day Rebecca was in for a routine appointment with her primary care doctor and casually mentioned how they hadn't been successful having children and how that was the last element that would make all their dreams come true. The doctor began telling my friend how "old" she was at thirty-seven to be trying to get pregnant and that she might already be past the time of being able to have babies without medical assistance.

"I was so surprised," Rebecca said, "because I assumed, like much of modern society, that lots of women have babies in their forties. All kinds of celebrities in the magazines are doing it, right?"

Well, the doctor quickly explained that that was why they were in the news—it's physically possible but statistically unusual. Plus, the doctor asked Rebecca if it had occurred to her that those celebrities have lots of money. They never talk about how much money they may have spent on fertility treatments. That's why they're still able to have children so late in life.

"I was taken aback and, frankly, quite alarmed," Rebecca recalled. "My doctor immediately referred me to an ob-gyn office that specializes in infertility, and they promptly assessed from my age that I had no time to lose and should probably even bypass the standard fertility drugs and go directly to the more aggressive methods."

She began attending a fertility clinic, little realizing that it would consume their lives physically, mentally, and emotionally for the next three years.

Rebecca and Waymond both had to go through weeks and weeks of testing to see if a cause for infertility could be determined, which would also indicate the extent of the fertility treatment they would need. "This was frustrating, because it became clear that every month that passed by was another precious chance lost," Rebecca said.

"And time was of the essence."

After the necessary battery of tests, it became clear that my friends would need to attempt the most intensive and technologically advanced infertility procedure—in vitro fertilization (IVF). "IVF is insanely expensive and is rarely covered by insurance," Rebecca said. Each case is different, and costs vary depending on many different factors, including the age of the woman, but each in vitro attempt for Rebecca and Waymond cost fifteen thousand to twenty thousand dollars.

The couple also was warned that it would be physically demanding for Rebecca, would require strong commitment from both spouses, and might put a strain on their marriage. "Nonetheless, it was absolutely clear to us that this was what we had to do to have the family we longed for," Rebecca said.

It took the couple three long years of disappointment after disappointment and a brutal five full attempts at IVF to finally be successful. "We were just about to give up trying and had accepted the reality of being childless," Rebecca recalled. "We were exhausted by the failures and dashed hopes. I was a physical wreck from the countless injections of hormones and steroids, and I could no longer face any more disappointment. Even the fertility doctors were not very enthusiastic about my continuing."

My friends went ahead with one more attempt only because they had already paid for most of the last procedure. "And, oh boy, were we successful on our halfhearted final attempt!" Rebecca said.

On February 14, 2003, Rebecca and Waymond's two fraternal sons, Ethan and Wyatt, were born.

"I guess until you've been there, or have had children already, many people would not understand our desire to have children," Rebecca said, adding that she can respect that some people thought they were crazy or at least self-indulgent to go through such elaborate machinations to have a baby. "But I'd also hope that those same people would have the sympathy and understanding to see the pure heartache a couple like us was willing to go through to fulfill a rather basic human desire to have a family," she said.

Their marriage was strengthened by the experience.

"We believe we're even closer now because of the amount of effort it took us to get through the ordeal," Rebecca said. "It forced us both to be really honest about our commitment and made it clear to us that our goals and willingness to sacrifice to achieve the dream of having our own children were exactly the same. And because of that, we now have two of the cutest little chubby, healthy baby boys ever born," my friend said. "We must be the happiest people on earth.

"It was all worth it."

Sheri and her husband, Jim, had been told they wouldn't

be able to have children because Jim had spinal meningitis as a teenager and therefore was probably sterile.

But early in their marriage, Sheri was attending a Bible study on Hannah and how she prayed for a child. "And I thought, *If God could do it for her, why not me?*" Sheri said. "So I prayed to the Lord, figured out my most fertile time, which was when Jim was on a business trip to Reno, went to visit him, and came home pregnant."

She also had twins—two daughters, Jennie and Kari.

And now they're proud grandparents to Jennie and Jason's daughter, Lexi.

Michael and I enjoy being "surrogate grandparents" to little Lexi, our great-niece. We have a blast shopping for baby clothes. They're so adorable. Especially girl clothes.

My best friend, Lana, a schoolteacher who married in her thirties and became an instant stepmom to her husband's teenage children, never raised small children but loves being a grandparent to her stepdaughter's children.

She and her husband, Michael, often babysit their two grandkids, Jacob and Colby, and have them spend the night. Recently when four-year-old Jacob came over to swim, he said to Michael, "Grandpa, you're my best buddy." Then he quickly added, "Daddy is too."

Jacob also informed Michael and Lana that he has two beds—one at his house and one at theirs.

"He considers the guest bedroom—which I have decorated kind of girly—his bedroom, girl stuff and all," Lana said. "Of course, he doesn't even notice that. He just knows that's where we keep his toy box—a boy toy box in his girl-stuff bedroom."

Christie, a new friend of mine who's been married just shy of fifteen years and is a mother of three, shares this funny story of how kids made a difference in her marriage.

"At first my honey and I thought we would enjoy a romantic stay at a nice little bed-and-breakfast after we had our kids, just like we did before they joined us," Christie recalled.

The couple waited until their eldest was two and his sister was three months before going off on a romantic getaway. Luckily, they were blessed with two sets of grandparents in town who were more than willing to watch the kids for the weekend. Only problem was, Christie was still breast-feeding three-month-old Cassidy.

"Even though she cooperated with Grandma and a bottle for those three days, I still couldn't let that milk build up the whole time we were away," Christie said, "so we took along a breast pump that my husband had cleverly rigged to plug into the lighter. That way we could stop between destinations and discreetly pull off the road for me to pump."

It worked, and the inventive couple just chalked it up to another difference between life with little people and the carefree existence they had before they became parents.

"Kids help you to focus on what's really important," Christie said. "Like not being materialistic. We went from college furniture to parent furniture seamlessly—especially when it came to our couch pillows. Everything we own is distressed, whether we bought it that way or not."

But this mom also asserts that it has been freeing to realize that she and her husband can't control everything—only God can.

"Greg and I have a new appreciation for the Beatitudes— blessings arise from so many things that seem bad by the world's standards," Christie said. "I would have never dreamed that it would be good for us to notice a chunk missing out of the side of my desk that someone tried to color in with a crayon. But if it helps us see how tightly we cling to our earthly treasures, then I can live with the dents and the dings."

Roanne and her husband, Ron, have three children who were very involved in sports growing up. "So even though coming into the marriage I didn't know the quarterback from the center, I eventually became pretty competent in the goings-on in the gym, on the football field, on the baseball diamond, and in the swimming pool," Roanne said. "I hate to admit it, but I actually came to love sports.

"To a point."

One Mother's Day Roanne's husband went shopping alone for her. "A scary proposition in itself," his wife said. "He's no shopper.

"His idea of holiday shopping for me is to follow our daughter around the mall with his checkbook," Roanne said. "But that Mother's Day he drove up so proudly, and in he came through the door, holding out my gift—a plant arrangement in a ceramic *basketball*!"

When asked if he has any kids, our friend Tony's response is, "Why are you asking?" If there's any trouble or they need money, they're his wife, Marianne's, kids. If things are going well, of course they're his.

But his wife of nearly thirty years doesn't mind. "This guy is a great father," Marianne said. "He's a softball coach, soccer helper—he'd like to coach, but who can understand those rules?—and teacher. All three of our children know their way around a toolbox, can build a fence, know how to fix almost anything in the home, and are all great cooks."

Debbie, my sis-in-law, says that one of the nicest things about growing up with children was traveling—whether for a short or long distance. "We would listen to them chatting away in the backseat of the car, overhearing some of the cute and goofy things they said, and then we would just look at each other and crack up," she said.

Her husband, Pastor Bob, would always make up weird, different words to familiar songs, and his sons caught on to it. "Just this last Father's Day, the boys took the music to a familiar gospel tune and turned it into a song about their dad and sang it at church," Debbie said. "It was very funny, but it also proved how much they love him."

Cindy and Mark, our Kansas pals, have this advice on kids: "Never try to outplan God. We waited ten years to have a child, and God laughed and gave us two at once. Twins—a pitcher and a catcher. Only they grew up and played soccer instead."

Gee, I'm getting the feeling there's something about twins . . .

Cindy says if you want a closer walk with God, become parents. And she offers the following:

The Top Five Reasons She Loves Being a Parent

1. My child's hug is pure love.
2. Parenting makes me stretch myself and become a better person.
3. Pure fun is cutting up with your kids—kid jokes, wrestling matches, water fights, doughy cookies.
4. Watching them grow is a gift I never want to give up.
5. What else would I do with twenty years of my life?

The Top Five Reasons She Wants Them to Go to College NOW

1. I want my free time back.
2. I want my free time back.
3. I want my free time back
4. I want my free time back.
5. I will have permanent arthritis and be sagging by the time I get them to leave.

Here's her personal prayer, which I'm sure most parents would echo: *Dear God, please help me be a good parent. Please help get Angel potty trained. Please don't let the tooth fairy forget the second night in a row, and please let us have a dollar left in the wallet. Please protect them from harm, and help them to seek positive friends and trust in God's love for all things. Please let them pass driver's ed, graduate from high school, and move out of the house and into college. Amen.*

Although Michael and I don't have children of our own—a personal choice we discussed and prayed about and which had to do with medical reasons—we have discovered over the years that marriage can be as rich and full without them, as have several of our married friends.

And when we feel the urge for a little mom-dad-child affection, we snuggle in for a group hug with Gracie.

Children's children are a crown to the aged,
and parents are the pride of their children.

Proverbs 17:6

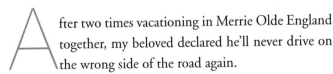

10

Together Wherever We Go
(or, Singin' in the Car)

One of the most common disrupters of marital bliss is the
choice of where to spend a vacation. What this country
needs is an ocean in the mountains.

Paul Sweeney

A fter two times vacationing in Merrie Olde England
together, my beloved declared he'll never drive on
the wrong side of the road again.

129

And I lovingly supported him in that decision.

It was the least I could do for our marriage. Can you say, Stress with a capital *S*? Make that three capital *S*'s.

As Michael carefully maneuvered his way down narrow one-lane roads—often having to back up and pull over as close to the edge as possible to let oncoming traffic pass (usually huge "lorries," or trucks)—around steep cliffs, and through confusing roundabouts with spokes pointing several directions, there was lots of noise in the car.

And none of it was singing.

Unlike most of our stateside vacations.

Michael and I have always liked singing in the car together on road trips. Usually, I'll begin a favorite show tune or old standard, and he'll quickly join in. My husband has a beautiful tenor voice, you see, and I love to hear him sing.

Certain show tune favorites from my sweetheart's pipes include "One Hand, One Heart" from *West Side Story*, *Godspell*'s "Prepare Ye the Way of the Lord," and "Bring Him Home" from *Les Miserables*.

Our singing in the car started in our dating days.

That was one of the things that made me realize Michael was "the one." (Although others, like our friends Chris and Steve, looked at us a little strangely as we ran through our entire Broadway repertoire during a double-date drive into the country for a picnic.)

I burst into "I Could Have Danced All Night" from *My Fair Lady*, Michael segued into "On the Street Where You Live," then we slid into *The King and I*'s "Shall We Dance?" and *every* song from *Oklahoma!*

Poor Chris couldn't stand it anymore and turned on the radio, but we continued to sing softly in the back seat together.

And I was well on my way to being smitten.

My friend Eve and her husband, Frank, who have been married thirty-three years, love car trips. "He drives; I talk," Eve said. "And when I don't talk, he worries."

A few years ago, shortly after she was diagnosed with breast cancer, Eve and Frank drove up to the mountains for the weekend. "I was in a bad mood all day," she recalled. "Actually, I was totally unlike my true self. In the past, I would 'nest' in the car with maps, articles, a picnic basket, and candles for the room and then do a continuous Chatty Cathy, which kept Frank happy—although I'm pretty sure he wasn't listening to all my chatter.

"But on this trip, I hadn't packed a picnic, maps, AAA books, travel articles, nada," Eve said. "And I wasn't talking. I was still angry about the cancer. Well, Frank started to worry: Why wasn't I talking? What was the matter? Where was the picnic basket?

"I quietly informed my husband that I wasn't Eve Dorf.

I was someone else who only looked like his wife, Eve. And I don't do maps or picnics. Nor do I talk." Eve kept up her pretense the entire drive up the interstate. "I got so tickled with keeping up this charade, I actually put myself in a good mood," she recalled, "and we had a wonderful weekend.

"Car trips are a good litmus test for marriage," Eve said, "and I think we passed the test."

Aunt Sharon and Uncle Jim, who live in Wisconsin, are both retired now and love to travel, especially by car. They probably take nine or ten road trips a year, with more than half of them to Tennessee to visit their grandkids.

"We're always looking for wildlife as we drive, 'cause I'm a wildlife buff," Sharon said. "I'm not a sleeper in the car, so I'm constantly looking at everything."

They also play little games in the car. Jim loves country western music, so he'll play a song from one of his favorite CDs and then quiz his wife on who's singing. "After a while, I don't want to answer," Sharon said.

Or they'll count cars from the different states each day. "Jim's not a real big talker in the car, or in anything, for that matter," his wife said. "I always have to be the one who does more talking."

Sharon's sister, my aunt Char, said that when her husband, Wayne, was alive, their vacations were always in the car.

132

"We would pick a direction and say, 'Okay, we'll travel for x number of miles and then take the first right,' and so on," Char recalled. "We wound up in a lot of nice little towns and cities that way. It was always very exciting to us—seeing a lot of different places that we had no intention of going to, or even knew about in the first place."

That works for Michael and me in the States too. For instance, for Michael's birthday last year, we decided to take a day trip to the ocean without a clear destination in mind. It was great. We have some of our best conversations in the car—times of dreaming and planning and connecting with one another without the distractions of home.

But in a different country, it's another story altogether.

Driving a small stick shift with the steering wheel on the right and the stick on the left on the *wrong* side of the mostly narrow roads turned my right-handed, normally sweet, Jekyll husband into a snarling Mr. Hyde—not the norm when he travels.

Of course, being the only man in a car with three women might have had a little something to do with it. (Michael's sister Sheri and our niece Kari accompanied us on this last trip, causing an Englishman friend to say to Michael, "You're a better man than I—vacationing with three women!")

Since I'm map and directionally impaired, everyone

thought it best that practical Sheri sit up front with Michael to navigate while Kari and I sat in the backseat. This worked pretty well. Most of the time.

Only problem was, this was Sheri's first time in England, and she was trying to read the map, watch which turnoff to take, *and* keep her eyes on the signs and scenery.

In Michael's defense, I have to admit that traffic was especially heavy. This was the day of a big horse race, not five miles from where we were, and the queen was attending. The roads were designed for horses and carriages, not for cars, and certainly not for the lorries that came whizzing past us.

Michael used all his acting ability to try to appear calm, but his sister saw through his façade when she noticed the hairs standing up on the backs of his hands. "I could feel his tension," Sheri recalled. "I think it even emanated to the sheep grazing nearby."

Sheep are a hillside staple in the Cotswolds, as are wonderful honey-colored cottages, quaint little towns with names like Stow-on-the-Wold and Bourton-on-the-Water, and gorgeous ancient churches that took our breath away. It was an idyllic day in the country.

Then we returned to Oxford.

Driving in the crowded university town is a nightmare in the best of times, which is why most people park in "car parks," or parking lots, on the outside of town and ride the bus in. We had chosen a rental car company on the outskirts of town precisely to avoid driving through the madness that is the city.

It only took one wrong turn.

As we approached Oxford, traffic became thicker. None of our maps detailed that particular area, so we were dependent on the ever-confusing road signs. Tension was already high when we came upon a roundabout that had seven or eight spokes leading off from it, and Sheri was still peering down at the map, trying to figure out which spoke to take, when Michael exited the roundabout.

From the backseat, I could immediately tell that we had taken the wrong exit and said, "Um . . ."

"What!" Michael asked in not very dulcet tones.

"Honey, I'm pretty sure you took the wrong turn. It was supposed to be the next one . . ."

Michael, who by now was at the zenith of his stress level, swerved the car off on a side road and braked. "If you think *you* can do better, why don't you drive?"

After a couple moments of tense silence, practical Sheri piped up, "She can't drive. She's not on the insurance." Ever the peacemaker, she added, "I certainly couldn't drive over here. There's too much to pay attention to. It's very stressful."

Lucky for us, we were close to the car rental agency or we

would have all imploded, taking the car with us. We heaved a collective sigh of relief once we turned the car in.

From then on, it was public transportation all the way.

We took the train into London, but that city certainly wreaked havoc on our already temporarily travel-strained relationship.

When we first planned a return trip to our beloved England—this time with Sheri and Kari—there was a special seven-day tour of London package for an affordable price that Michael, Sheri, and Kari wanted to take.

Having lived in England and visited the capital city countless times, I was a tad hesitant. "Honey, I think seven days is a little too long in London. You really can do the whole city in four days. Tops. What would you think if we spent seven days in the lush, green countryside and four days in the city instead?"

But my cultured Renaissance man, who didn't get to see *any* of London on our first trip—we were in England when 9/11 happened—wanted as much time as possible in this historic, culture-filled cosmopolitan city.

And when Michael, Sheri, and Kari looked at all the sights that were included in our seven-day group tour—Buckingham Palace, Westminster Abbey, St. Paul's Cathedral, the Tower of London, Windsor Castle, the National Gallery, the British Library, the British Museum, Covent Garden, a trip down

136

the Thames to Greenwich, and *more*, they all agreed that they didn't want to miss a single thing.

So I graciously conceded since it was their first time. (What's that old *Star Trek* line? "The needs of the many outweigh the needs of the few, or the one"?)

Really. I was quite gracious about it when we booked the tour. (Although I did insist, since we were flying all that way already, that we had to spend at least a couple days in the countryside at the beginning of the trip.)

Culture vulture Michael researched for months to determine the "must-see" sights not on the tour, and we all unwittingly agreed that we should fill the free time not scheduled with the already-full tour.

Insanity or stupidity? Either one will do.

It was about midway through London that all my grace flew out the window of our fourth-floor hotel room. Fifty-nine narrow stairs up and down every day with no elevator—or "lift."

> *It was about midway through London that all my grace flew out the window of our fourth-floor hotel room.*

You know how fussy babies can be when they're tired? They wail and scream those deep-lunged, red-faced cries to let moms know, "I need my nap!"

Add 46 years and 150 pounds—give or take a few—and

you have me. But our schedule was so tight, there was no time for napping, resting, or reading the whole time we were in London. Although once or twice after a long tour day, I managed to steal a few minutes of rest sitting on the floor of Sheri and Kari's hotel room, reading the *London Times*. (I didn't have the energy to hike up the remaining thirteen steps to our room on the top floor.)

The morning we visited magnificent St. Paul's Cathedral, we were given a twenty-minute break to climb to the top of the dome—all 530 steps. That's 44 flights of stairs one way. What were they *thinking*? We needed several hours and a picnic. No one in our foursome even bothered to attempt it, including Michael, whose legs were also starting to wear out by then.

Instead, we spent the twenty minutes having a cup of tea and browsing in the gift shop for postcards.

The tour agency we used, while wonderful in many ways, doesn't allow scheduled time for shopping. Sightseeing, exploring, and getting to know the locals is their thing. All of which I love. But fifteen-to-twenty-minute increments to shop isn't enough. Especially when you have to buy souvenirs for everyone back home.

So now we had to add shopping into our unscheduled "downtime," in addition to fancy afternoon tea and the theater. (We got to see three absolutely fabulous shows in the

West End: *My Fair Lady, Les Miserables*—our favorite musical—and *The Mousetrap*, which has been running continuously for more than fifty years!) *That* part of our London experience I loved.

Part of the problem is simply that I'm not a big-city girl.

Never have been. Wait, I take that back. I guess I was for a brief period in my early twenties, when I was young, single, and stationed overseas. But that was more than two decades ago.

Things change.

Now I can only take so much of crowds, noise, and concrete. And after four days of big-city living, I was ready to escape to the bucolic countryside.

I *need* pastoral. Give me a rolling green hill, a couple of sheep here and there, a quaint little cottage or two, a charming B & B, and a village pub where I can get some nice fish and chips, and I'm a blissful Anglophile.

Plus, I'm not a history buff like my husband.

I don't care which king in the twelfth century did what, or who fought whom, or who discovered what: "Oh, that's the tower where they beheaded Henry's wives? Nice. Interesting. What's next?"

But Michael adores history and had spent months before our vacation immersing himself in English history, and in particular, London history, so he was eager to see and learn about everything. And didn't feel he had *enough* time in the city to see everything.

In fact, both Michael and Kari had a great time and can't wait to go back. Michael said he needs *at least* four more days in the city to see everything he wants to see.

At the end of our trip, an exhausted Sheri and I agreed that if we never saw London again, that would be okay.

Although now that a little more time has passed, Sheri says she'd visit the capital again, but only for a couple of days, on *her* schedule. "Like fine wine, the trip gets better with age," she admitted.

I agree. Now that I've gotten my R & R—rest and reading time—I've relented and told my sweetheart I'll be happy to return with him for a couple days at the beginning or end of our next England trip—if for nothing else than to see some more great theater in the West End.

Just as long as we don't have to climb fifty-nine steps to our hotel room.

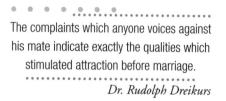

The complaints which anyone voices against his mate indicate exactly the qualities which stimulated attraction before marriage.

Dr. Rudolph Dreikurs

11

The Nagging Gene Revisited
(or, Are You *Listening* to Me?)

I have learned that only two things are necessary to keep one's
wife happy. First, let her think she's having her way.
And second, let her have it.

Lyndon Baines Johnson

n my first book, *Dated Jekyll, Married Hyde*, I talked about
a genetic trait common to many women that doesn't usually kick in until after marriage—the nagging gene. And

when I did radio and TV interviews to promote that book, it was funny how that was the chapter most of the male hosts wanted to discuss.

Wonder why.

With a few more years of wisdom under my marital belt now, I decided that I should revisit this mostly feminine genetic trait.

Let me say right up front that I never planned on being a nag. Ever. During my years and years as a single woman, whenever I saw women nagging their husbands, I found it unattractive and unappealing.

And such a cliché.

But you know what? The reason something becomes a cliché is usually because it's grounded in truth.

Still, I vowed that I would *never* become the *N* word. Then I pledged to love, honor, and cherish and promptly broke my premarital vow. "I do" quickly morphed into "Dear, did you _____ [fill in the blank: take out the trash? call your mother? clean out the gutters?]."

My biggest nagging area relates to the phone. Michael's job entails his being on the phone all day long, so when he gets home, he hates to use it. Therefore, I'm the one who always answers it and acts as the social secretary who makes the obligatory calls to friends and family.

a kiss is still a kiss

There are times, however, when Michael needs to make the call—particularly if it involves car repairs, home improvements, or other guy kinds of stuff that I'm not good at. And when he doesn't call promptly or he forgets, my nagging gene comes out in full force.

"Honey, don't forget to call so-and-so about the car before they close." "Honey, have you called that gardening place about an estimate yet?" "Darling, it's getting late. Don't you think you'd better call your grandmother?"

It's not that I want to be a nag; it's just that he forgets if I don't remind him.

My writing pal Christie says nagging is more unattractive than morning breath. And as a dewy-eyed young single woman, she too vowed that she would never resort to such ugly attempts at wifely influence. "How could you keep a man by being a nag, anyway?" she wondered at the time.

"I do" quickly morphed into "Dear, did you [fill in the blank: take out the trash? call your mother? clean out the gutters?]."

But that was before she undertook another set of vows—the matrimonial kind—where the focus soon became not on keeping the man but on keeping her sanity.

"Ninety-seven percent of the time, my Gregory seems too good to be true," Christie asserted. "But in the wake of his hormonal eclipse—I think guys have hormonal fluctuations too!—he turns into a guy who makes Stonewall Jackson look like a pushover. After running smack into that other 3 percent of my husband's stubbornness-incarnate resolve, I appreciated one of my areas of concentration in grad school even more," she said. "The study of persuasion."

Michael's sister Debbie leaves notes for her husband, Bob. "That way he doesn't have to say a word, but he knows exactly what I want done—laundry, vacuuming, whatever," my sister-in-law said. "If he has a chance, he'll do it. If not, I'll leave another note another day."

Michael and I started the note thing early in our marriage but have gotten out of the habit the past few years. I think it's time to reinstitute it though. Thanks, Deb!

Unfortunately, it's not a perfect solution. Debbie says that Bob will often say to her, "Just tell me what you want me to do," but when she does, he considers it nagging. Go figure.

This extends into their social lives as well.

"I'll tell Bob about a function I want the two of us to attend, and he says, 'Sure,'" Debbie related. "A week before the event, I'll remind him, and he'll say, 'Sure.' Two days before the event I'll remind him again, and he'll say, 'Sure.' The day before the event, I'll remind him, and he'll say, 'Sure.' The day of the event, I'll remind him, and he'll say, 'What event? When did I ever say I'd go to that?'!"

Naturally, Debbie finds that very frustrating. But at least Bob usually goes to the event.

Sheri says she never nags. "If it's not important to me, I'll let it go. If it is, I'll take care of it," Sheri said. "There are no honey-do lists in this house. If we do honey-do stuff—normally big projects—we do them together because it's important."

Lately, I've been trying to be more like my sister-in-law and less of a nag.

But even Sheri, the non-nag, has run into difficulties getting her husband, Jim's, attention on occasion.

See, Jim's a big television sports guy, particularly golf, and he enters another zone—the sports zone—where he can't hear sounds around him. His eyes remain fixed and staring at the entertainment box before him.

Sheri used to stand in front of him, tap her nose with her finger, and say, "Look at me." Other times, she'd place her hands on his head, physically turn his face to her, and say, "Look at me!" But over the years, she's learned to wait until a commercial to talk to her husband. "I accommodate that because I realize he's like that, so why get upset about it?" Sheri said. "Just work around it."

Sometimes that doesn't always work.

Take my aunt Char, who lives in Illinois.

One weekend, she took her then-eight-year-old son Chris

to a book fair, and as she bent down to tell him not to touch, she tripped on the raised sidewalk and fell, landing hard on a cement stair. She remembers hearing her son yelling, "Mom, Mom!" but it was as if it was from a long distance.

"I kept passing out," Char recalled. "But then I finally felt a little better, and we went inside to the book fair, with my not having a clue as to how I looked—which must have been pretty bad because people kept saying, 'Oh my gosh, are you okay?' They wanted to call the rescue squad for me, but I was more concerned about how that would impact Chris—that it might frighten him—so I said no."

After buying a book for Chris, and feeling worse by the minute, Char decided it was time to head home. "We lived only five minutes away," she said, "but it took us twenty minutes to get home because I had to keep pulling over because of the dizziness."

When mom and son finally arrived home, Char's husband, Wayne, was sitting in the living room with his back to her, caught up in his favorite TV show. "As I approached his chair, I said, 'I think I broke my arm, and I think I have to go to the hospital,'" Char recalled.

Unhearing, or simply oblivious, Wayne never turned, just sat and kept watching his program. Finally Char faced him and said, "Do we have to wait until tomorrow, or can we go to the hospital tonight?"

Looking up at last and seeing his bruised and disheveled wife, Wayne was out of his chair like a shot. He drove Char to the emergency room, where they discovered she had broken and dislocated her arm.

"We laughed about that for many years," Char said. (His obliviousness, not her broken arm.)

But to be fair, it's not just husbands who get this way.

When I'm caught up in a good book, I tune out everything around me—Michael, Gracie, whistling teakettles . . . The only thing that brought me up short once was the smoke alarm after Michael burned some bacon in the kitchen.

Oops.

The Japanese have a word for it. It's judo—the art of conquering by yielding. The Western equivalent of judo is, "Yes, dear."

J. P. McEvoy

12

The Kitchen Connection (or, Too Many Cooks Spoil the Broth)

When a man talks to you about his mother's cooking, pay no
attention, for between the ages of 12 and 21, a boy can eat
large quantities of anything and never feel it.

Sarah Tyson Rorer

Michael and I cannot work in the kitchen together.

Most of the time, that is. Now and then, if it's just making snacks or something easy, it's not a problem. He chops the vegetables while I get the drinks and chips or cheese and crackers.

But an actual meal? Forget it.

We're always getting in each other's way.

And it makes me crazy when I'm cooking something and he comes in and watches me. Eventually, I'm sure he's going to suggest a better way of sautéing the mushrooms and onions or seasoning the stew.

Sometimes he does. But other times, he just wants to *be* with me. Aw.

Every year since we bought our cute little 1950s ranch house—which I prefer to think of as "cottage style"—with the original kitchen (read, no dishwasher, garbage disposal, or counter space), I've declared, "I'm NOT going to have Thanksgiving dinner here."

Yet several years running, we did.

The first year, we were so thrilled to be in "our home" that we invited *both* sides of the family over for Thanksgiving. We had the dining space to fit everyone—Michael brought a big, bulky table with two leaves to the marriage, plus we had a card table for kids—so that wasn't a problem.

a kiss is still a kiss

Cooking in that antiquated kitchen was.

Can you say, no room?

No function?

And of course, since it was our first Thanksgiving in our new home, I wanted to make everything just perfect. We bought a huge turkey—a twenty-four-pounder, I think—which fit nicely in our brand-new oven.

The problem was counter space.

There wasn't any.

We knew a card table wouldn't support the weight of that big bird, so Michael had to bring in an industrial-strength folding table from the garage and set it up in the cramped kitchen.

Everyone wanted to help out: my mom was trying to stir the gravy, my sister-in-law was checking on the rolls, my sister was nuking her creamed peas, Michael was trying to slice the turkey, and I was losing my mind.

You wouldn't think it would be so hot in November, would you? Put five people together in a tiny kitchen, with one of them being the menopausal, hot-flashin' woman of the house, and by the time I sat down, my face was as bright as the cranberry sauce.

The following year we did Thanksgiving again but for a smaller group.

And the next time we hosted Turkey Day at our home,

Michael hit upon what he thought was a great solution: *he* would cook the Thanksgiving dinner. Not me.

Then I wouldn't get stressed. But my honey had an ulterior motive.

The previous year—remembering how crowded and difficult it had been that first Thanksgiving—when everyone kept offering to help me, I kept shooing them out of the kitchen. Including Michael.

"Go visit and entertain our guests," I lovingly hissed at him.

Now, if there's anything Michael hates to do, it's visit. Making small talk is not his forte. Think fingernails on a chalkboard.

He'd much rather be doing something. Keeping busy. Accomplishing something.

Michael can't sit still for very long. It drives him crazy. Plus, he loves to cook.

While I, on the other hand, love to visit, am the queen of small talk, and have no problem sitting still. So it made perfect, logical sense to him that we trade places.

He could cook and keep busy—which he loves—and I could visit and entertain the family—which I love.

Only thing he forgot to take into consideration was how important it was for me to cook. To show my family that I could do it.

a kiss is still a kiss

See, it's like this.

Michael and I are an atypical couple in many ways.

He likes to sew; I don't.

He likes to do craft projects—from scrapbooking to rubber-stamping to making banners for church. I don't have a crafty bone in my body or the patience for it.

So whenever anyone comes over, they all ooh and aah over Michael's beautiful handiwork gracing our home. From gorgeous quilts on the wall, to slipcovers on the chair, to cushions on our antique church pew, and most recently, to oil paintings.

I can't sew a stitch—and have no desire to. And as for painting, my dad had all the talent in the family for that.

And that's fine with me. Truly.

Because my talent, my gift, is writing, and I've pretty much known that most of my life.

Another creative passion of mine is decorating. Michael may make all the original art, but *I'm* the one who knows exactly how and where to display it. But you know what? I also love to cook. When I have the time—which is rare these days.

So when people come over to eat, they naturally assume that Michael cooked the meal. After all, he makes a killer lasagna, wonderful chili, and all those quilts.

We've hit upon a solution that works for both of us, however: we'll switch off years cooking the Thanksgiving turkey. He'll do it one year; I'll do it the next.

Sheri and Jim don't have problems in the kitchen.

"We have a clear division of duties when it comes to cooking," my sister-in-law said. "He barbecues; I do the side dishes. I chop the veggies and do the potatoes. He's the expert on meat or anything grilled. For breakfast, he cooks and I clean. Jim surprises me with breakfast a lot. He'll come wake me and say, 'Breakfast is served.'"

Before marrying Steve, my girlfriend Chris never cooked.

The first time she cooked Steve a meal, they weren't dating yet. They were "just friends," although Chris wanted more, and she definitely wanted to impress Steve. She microwaved frozen chicken cordon bleu and served it with canned green beans, tater tots, and toasted garlic bread.

"So this is how you cook?" Steve asked.

"Sure," Chris replied. "This is good."

"No, this is all packaged," the man of her dreams told her.

Thankfully, Steve didn't let her lack of culinary expertise deter him from falling in love. Besides, Chris was a quick learner. Now she makes all the food. From scratch. And saves a tremendous amount of money doing so.

Katie, a mutual friend who lives in the countryside near the beautiful Napa Valley of California, taught her how.

She tried to teach me too. But it didn't take.

Our church friends Tony and Marianne are approaching their third decade of marriage. And after all this time, Marianne says she has come to understand, and be patient with, many things.

"If I'm cooking and he says, 'Why don't you let me help you?' what he really means is, 'Let me do it my way,'" Marianne related. "After his cooking episode is finished, and he's 'done cleaning' the kitchen, then I step in and clean the kitchen.

"He must have some sort of anti-see-the-mess radar. When I ask him, 'What about the mess in the kitchen?' he says, 'What mess? I already cleaned it.' Or his favorite line—'The kids did it,'" she said.

Then the long-married Marianne asks her beloved, "Honey, how did you get ketchup on the ceiling?"

Tony decided to respond to his wife's comments point by point.

"After all these years of marriage, I haven't learned a thing," he said. "Like when I try to help in the kitchen: if I think I've found a better or faster way of doing something, isn't it worth a look? See, honey, I can juggle potatoes and peel them at the same time!

"And thank goodness for her CCD [compulsive cleaning

disorder]. I wiped up all the big spots. Besides, the kids are just going to tear it up soon anyway," Tony said.

Also, he knows Marianne will enjoy "detailing" her kitchen. "Kind of like how I like to clean my tools after a job," Tony said. "I wouldn't dream of taking that away from her.

"Oh, and, honey, I swear that ketchup has been there for weeks. I didn't do it; the kids did."

She watches over the affairs of her household.

Proverbs 31:27

13

The Weaker Sex

In society it is etiquette for ladies to have the best chairs and get

handed things. In the home the reverse is the case.

That is why ladies are more sociable than gentlemen.

Virginia Graham

Babies and husbands have a lot in common.
They both need lots of TLC when they're sick.
My aunt Sharon recounted this story of Jack and

Joan, her brother-in-law and sister-in-law, who have been married more than forty years.

One Friday night just a few years into their marriage, Jack came down with a terrible toothache. He managed to cope with it that evening, but come Saturday morning he told his wife, "I really can't stand this; you're going to have to find a dentist for me."

When a man gets sick, the whole world stops.

Since they didn't have a steady dentist, Joan began looking in the phone book for one. She called a few, but no one was open on a Saturday. "Jack was being a bear," my aunt Sharon recalled. "When a man gets sick, the whole world stops."

Suddenly Joan had a great idea. She remembered that she had some leftover medicated solution for her kids, so she said out loud to herself, "I have some gum balm I'll use."

Joan was in the kitchen and Jack was in the living room of their long apartment when he shouted in to her, "I heard that guy Balm is a real good dentist."

"That's not a *dentist*," Joan yelled back. "I happen to have some *gum balm* from the kids when they were teething."

The balm did the trick nicely and held Jack over until Monday morning.

My email pal Roanne sent me this about her husband, Ron.

"I was slow to figure out [my husband's response to pain and illness], but my first clue should have been how unglued he always was in the labor and delivery rooms," Roanne said. "If I had a pain, so did he. He would have to leave the room when the needles came in. Over the years it has become apparent that the man doesn't do illnesses well. If I had a rash, he thought maybe he was getting one.

"A headache for me? He would feel one coming on," Roanne said. "And the day I had an ovarian cyst removed, I swear he was beginning to hold his side. So over the course of many years, I have become immune to his 'disorder' and pretty much ignore his aches and pains. I know—not very nice of me. But in the last couple of years, he actually has begun laughing about it with me."

Over the years it has become apparent that the man doesn't do illnesses well. If I had a rash, he thought maybe he was getting one.

About five years ago, however, Roanne woke up in the middle of the night to find her husband crawling around on all fours.

"What *are* you doing?" she asked.

He claimed he had a stomachache.

"And you woke me up for a stomachache? For Pete's sake, get a grip and get back to bed," his loving wife said. "You'll feel better in the morning."

"Well, I'm ashamed to say it didn't get better," Roanne recalled, "and I ended up taking him to the emergency room— he was admitted with a kidney stone. I won't win any wife of the year awards for that one."

I had a similar experience with Michael not long ago.

His beloved sister Sheri had recently been diagnosed with lymphoma, which included a baseball-size tumor in her groin area that the doctors were shrinking with chemotherapy.

Shortly after his sister's diagnosis, Michael came into our room a little hesitantly one night when I was reading in bed. "Honey, I didn't want to say anything, but I feel something a little strange in my groin area—some kind of lump that wasn't there before," he said.

Certain that it was just sympathy pains because Michael is especially close to Sheri, and because he, like Roanne's husband, has a "disorder" when it comes to illness and pain, which over the years I too had become somewhat immune to, I felt the "lump."

"Oh, that's just a muscle, honey," I said. "I don't think it's anything to worry about. But if you're concerned, why don't you call the doctor?"

a kiss is still a kiss

He was. And he did.

Turns out he had a hernia that required major surgery.

There went my wife of the year award.

I felt awful and tried to make it up to my beloved by being the best nurse I could.

The good news was that since Michael's recuperation co-incided with Sheri's second round of chemo, he was able to accompany his sister to her treatments a couple times, which meant a lot to him. And her.

Both of them are now doing well.

And so am I.

The day after our first wedding anniversary, I was diagnosed with breast cancer. Needless to say, this turned our lives upside down. I won't go into all of it here, because I already talked about it briefly in *Dated Jekyll, Married Hyde* and detailed the whole experience in *Thanks for the Mammogram!*

What I will say, however, is that a life-threatening illness like that really puts those "in sickness and in health" marriage vows to the test. And I'm happy to say that we passed with flying, albeit a little shaky, colors. Michael took great care of me, and I've now been cancer free for more than twelve years. Thank you, God.

Our dear friends Jan and Mike also have been through the life-threatening illness scare. Jan has Crohn's disease, an inflammatory bowel disease that affects the small and large intestines. Crohn's is a chronic, debilitating illness that causes severe pain.

"Mike has been very supportive, *very* understanding," Jan said. "He's the kind of person who looks for solutions when there's a problem. He always looks on the positive side. For me, I'd probably be more of a downer, the 'woe is me, oh what are we going to do?' type," she admitted. "But Mike can say, 'I'm so sorry this has happened. Okay, what can we do about it?' And that's a blessing."

Jan said she learned through her illness that she's always been someone who feels she has to prove herself, to show that she's good enough. "I was scared that Michael was going to see this different person now and he wasn't going to like it," she said.

Once, during the height of a Crohn's flare-up shortly before dawn, Jan woke up distraught. "I was so emotional and so sick," she recalled. "I got my clothes on and said, 'I'm going to take a drive.' And even though it was a workday, Mike said, 'I'm going to go with you.'" It was very early in the morning, and the couple drove into the hills and watched the sunrise. "He was there beside me, just loving me, letting me have my emotional time, and letting things get back to normal," Jan said.

At another point, my poor friend was losing her hair and had blisters all over her mouth. "I felt unclean and untouchable," Jan recalled. "And Mike came to kiss me, but I put my

a kiss is still a kiss

hand up and said, 'No, I'm all icky.' He plowed right through that, kissed me, and said, 'I love you. *Now*. Today. I just love you for you.'"

Her husband's tender actions created a very powerful bond between the couple. "He showed me God's love in a very real, very tangible way," Jan said, "which is so important in marriage, because marriage is a holy sacrament. The fact that God used my illness to show me his love, his unconditional love, through Mike in a marriage relationship that *he* had ordained for us . . . 'Wonderful' doesn't even begin to say it. It was so much more than that."

Jan had successful surgery for her Crohn's several years ago and is now in remission.

Okay, so maybe husbands tend to whimper a little more than we do when they're sick. But when their wives need them, they step up to the "in sickness and in health" plate and carry the load with love and compassion.

Both Jan and I can vouch for that.

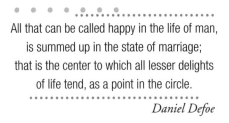

All that can be called happy in the life of man,
is summed up in the state of marriage;
that is the center to which all lesser delights
of life tend, as a point in the circle.

Daniel Defoe

14
His Relaxing Needs, Her Relaxing Needs

May I wish for you the knowledge . . . that Marriages do not Take Place, they are made by hand; that there is always an element of discipline involved; that however perfect the honeymoon, the time will come, however brief it is, when you will wish she would fall downstairs and break a leg. That goes for her too. But the mood will pass, if you give it time.

Raymond Chandler

Michael and I like to have a Boxing Day at least once a year.

No, I'm not talking about putting on the gloves and duking it out. In our house, Boxing Day means something entirely different.

In England, there's a centuries-old tradition called Boxing Day, celebrated the day after Christmas. Initially—in fine houses—this meant boxing up all the leftovers and giving them to the poor and then giving the servants the day off. But some Americans (who didn't have servants) adapted it to mean a relaxing, restful time at home without outside interruptions.

We think every couple needs a Boxing Day from the world occasionally. Lock the doors, pull the blinds, unplug the phone, and burrow in, ignoring the rest of the world.

Think of it as an at-home vacation. Without the expense or travel time.

We've tried to maintain at least some of the English tradition by observing our Boxing Day the day after Christmas, but we have run into a few snags.

Especially when friends or relatives, who often have that day off from work, decide to drop by for an unannounced visit in the midst of their after-Christmas-sale shopping and see both our cars in the driveway.

The second time this happened, Michael said, "We need to

a kiss is still a kiss

drive one of our cars down the street and park it somewhere else and then walk back to our house so they'll think we're gone somewhere."

It was a great, romantic idea, but he'd forgotten one important thing.

Keys.

You see, we've given a few family members keys to our house in case of an emergency. Or for those times when we go out of town and they need to come in and feed Gracie or water the plants. Or for the occasional time when we need to give them something but don't have time to run it over to their house before some social engagement. This way, they can run by at their leisure when we're gone and pick it up.

Not a problem. Usually.

Until the year we forgot that we'd told my mom we'd leave out a gift that needed to be exchanged on the table for her.

Michael had parked his car down the street as planned, and we'd pulled all the drapes, unplugged the phone, and settled in for some romantic afternoon cuddling when suddenly we heard the front door open and my mom's voice greeting Gracie.

"I knew I should have fixed that broken doorbell," Michael said.

Mom had knocked, but we hadn't heard her, so seeing just

the one car, she thought we weren't home and used her key to come in and pick up the package to exchange.

The next year we celebrated Boxing Day in a nearby English B & B instead.

My brother-in-law Jim enjoys watching sports on TV, and for some unknown reason that his wife, Sheri, cannot fathom, he wants her to be there with him while he's watching. "He doesn't want to talk to me or anything; he just wants me there," Sheri said.

So my sister-in-law thought she would take up an activity she could do while sitting in the living room. "I took up cross-stitching, and it's a habit I love to this day. So I got something I loved out of it."

Rene, an email pal, has been married to Mike for twenty-seven years. Early on in their marriage, they used to have a frequent argument about relaxing. They both worked forty hours a week and would come home dog tired every night. With three kids in the house, there was always dinner to be made, dinner dishes to be cleaned up, etc.

Rene says a typical night went like this: Mike and Rene would walk in the door together. Mike would head to the family room, sit in his favorite recliner, put his feet up, and watch the news.

Rene, on the other hand, would go in the kitchen and immediately start making dinner. As she was fixing dinner, she'd get angrier and angrier because *she* would be working and he'd be relaxing.

What's wrong with this picture? We both worked all day. How come he gets to relax and I don't? she would think.

Rene would get so angry that she would refuse to ask for help, even though she didn't really need help—it was the *principle* of the thing: she thought she should *have* help. She figured Mike should be able to read her mind and she shouldn't have to *ask* for help. To her, it was only obvious that she was tired too after being on her feet all day. And she was still on her feet—in the kitchen, working alone!

To get Mike's attention, Rene would slam the cupboard doors as she prepared dinner. Subtle, quiet slamming at first. Then the slamming would slowly intensify and get louder and more frequent until finally Mike would call out, "Do you need help in there?"

By this time, Rene was too mad to admit she needed help— even though she didn't really need help, it being the principle of the thing and all. Her feeling was that Mike shouldn't have to ask if she needed help. He should know she needed help. He should be able to read her mind.

That was her first mistake. Husbands can't read minds— especially their wives'.

Then came the inevitable discussion. "You think *your* job is more important than mine," Rene pouted. "Therefore, you just assume that because I'm the wife, I should come home after working eight hours and make dinner."

The cupboard slamming went on for years until it had finally run its course. One evening in about their fifteenth year of marriage, Mike and Rene finally had it out.

Rene had to admit defeat. Her husband couldn't read her mind. And her cupboard slamming—passive-aggressive behavior—wasn't accomplishing a single thing. Mike said, "If you need my help, just ask."

Whoa. That was too simple, Rene thought. *Just ask? No way.*

Besides, she shouldn't have to ask. He should just know. No, wait. They'd tried that. For fifteen years. It didn't work.

Mike was true to his word. If she asked for his help, he helped. And sometimes she didn't even have to ask. He would just *offer* to help.

Amazing.

Now their evening scenario goes like this: Mike and Rene come home from work. Usually Rene makes dinner and Mike cleans up. But sometimes Mike makes dinner. Whoever makes dinner, the other one cleans up.

They now have equal time in the kitchen.

170

Oh, and about those three kids? They grew up. One of them has his own house and does his own dishes. The other two are always gone, or they disappear like magic right after dinner. However, they do chores around the house during the day when Mike and Rene are at work.

"So now it's just like before when the kids were little and we did everything in the evenings," Rene said. "Only now they're big and we do everything . . . Hey! What's wrong with this picture?"

My girlfriend Cindy, who lives in Kansas, has a husband who's a golfing addict, so she made up a couple of top five lists about her husband's relaxation obsession.

The Top Five Reasons Cindy Hates Golf

1. It takes away from "our time."
2. It takes away from family time.
3. It's on TV all year round.
4. He forgets he's on the planet when he's playing or watching.
5. It's his weekly fix.

The Top Five Reasons She Puts Up with Golf

1. He needs his weekly relaxation fix.
2. He's more fun at the lake sailing Saturday afternoon if he plays eighteen holes Saturday morning.
3. If he gets four hours of Saturday morning golf, I get four hours of afternoon movie time with the girls.
4. Better chasing balls around a groomed pasture than women around a bar.
5. It's my compromise for the marriage.

June, my septuagenarian pen friend, and her husband, Red, always liked to go camping, walking in the desert, or following trails in the mountains or old logging roads.

"We discovered that we could have alone time yet still be together," June said. She always brought along a book bag crammed with books, a journal, pens, colored markers, a Bible, and a notebook, and Red brought his favorite walking stick and a battery-powered radio.

"Both of us felt free to walk alone, to read, to listen to birds singing or the wind rustling the tree leaves, and to watch the squirrels and chipmunks," June recalled. "Away from home, job cares, and family concerns, both of us seemed to communicate better. It was easier to really talk to one another.

"Voicing our deep personal concerns had always been difficult for both of us," she said. "I regret this and know I could probably have found help for us to learn to share our thoughts and feelings—both of us would have been better for that."

Another pen friend, Pam, and her husband, Jack, met in church when he was in the Navy and on his way to Iceland. The young couple wrote back and forth for the thirteen months he was stationed on that cold island, fell in love via airmail, and were married a few months after Jack returned to the States.

They've now been married thirty-four years.

Pam learned through all those airmail letters that her husband-to-be was a real car fiend. "If it's got four wheels and a motor, Jack wants to see it, touch it, listen to it, and smell the exhaust," she said. "His favorite thing is watching about forty-five stock cars scream around a racetrack at two hundred plus miles per hour.

"I can take it or leave it," Pam said. "I appreciate the work that goes into the 'birth' of a stock car—the motor that spins at nine thousand rpms for a five-hundred-mile race, the spiffy paint scheme, the driver, the owner, the whole race team. But frankly, I'd rather be reading a good book."

You and me both, Pam.

But the couple has learned how to compromise.

When it comes time for an extended vacation, they've devised a good system.

"We'll look at the NASCAR Winston Cup race schedule, decide which race we'd like to attend, and plan our vacation around that time period," Pam said. "Then we check out what else is going on in that area. Since most Winston Cup races are in the southeastern United States, there's not much of a problem with making me happy. There's usually something historical, which I dearly love, or other activities that can be *my* part of the vacation."

One year, the couple flew into Birmingham, Alabama, on a Tuesday and drove up to Nashville and attended the Dove Awards. "That was *my* part of the vacation," Pam said. "I'm a Christian music junkie."

Wednesday of that same week, they happened to walk by the place where they used to tape the Wildhorse Saloon segments for TV—line dancing, country style. "We found out they were taping that evening, so yee-haw, we went out and bought a cowboy hat and boots for me (Jack wears boots all the time, so dad-gum, he was ready), and we were all duded up for the taping that night. Not that we actually got out on the dance floor, but it was great fun to sit there and watch."

Friday, they drove back down to Talladega, Alabama, just in time for a weekend full of car races. "It's been my experience that if there isn't a race going on at the racetrack in question,

Jack will find one locally where there *is* something going on," Pam said. "In the South, somebody's always racing a car somewhere—especially on a Saturday night."

Sunday was the big Winston Cup race. "Jack can't figure out why I usually take a book and read it during the race," Pam said. "I guess I just need something more to do than watch little cars go around and around in a circle for three hours. He thinks I'm crazy for paying all that money for a seat and then reading a book instead of watching the race."

And that's how they compromise and do a vacation that's acceptable for both of them.

But for their landmark twenty-fifth anniversary, Pam asked if just once they could go someplace where there wasn't a racetrack. So they went to Alaska.

"I figure we'll finally get to see Hawaii as soon as they build a Winston Cup track there."

Learn the wisdom of compromise, for it is better to bend a little than to break.

Jane Wells

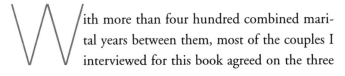

15

The Three Secrets
to a Happy Marriage

Chains do not hold a marriage together. It is threads, hundreds
of tiny threads, which sew people together through the years.

Simone Signoret

With more than four hundred combined marital years between them, most of the couples I interviewed for this book agreed on the three

177

secrets to a happy marriage: Communicate. Communicate. Communicate.

But it's not always an easy thing, since we're dealing with the opposite sex and those hormonal brain barriers.

I submit that when a man and woman talk to one another, particularly if they're married, the message is received by the ear but gets confused—or lost—in the communication processing center in the brain.

When women talk to one another, it's a straight shot from reception of the message to understanding. But when a man says something to a woman, or vice versa, the message is received, enters the brain's communication center, is sent to the verbal information maze, and must then make its way through the confusing maze to come out the other side of it to understanding.

Most of the time, however, the message takes the wrong path, gets lost in the maze, and begins running in frustrating circles from one dead end to another.

Most of the time, however, the message takes the wrong path, gets lost in the maze, and begins running in frustrating circles from one dead end to another.

My friend Jan is a perfect example. One day she said she was "jabbering on about something at warp speed" to her husband, Carl, "spitting out disjointed words."

"Carl got that glazed look in his eyes while trying to smile patiently," Jan recalled. "I know he's confused and can't process what I'm trying to say when that look appears. Finally he just gave up and said, 'What are you talking about?' At that point, I was so frustrated I said, 'Can't you hear what I *mean*?'"

And yet her best friend, Jeanne, hears what she means despite what she says. "And I don't have to use nearly as many words," Jan said.

It's that girl connection.

Once in their forty-year marriage, Uncle Jim was working second shift at the factory and Aunt Sharon was working either first or third shift, so they didn't get to see each other much.

"Communication was pretty sad," Sharon recalled. So one night she decided to do something special and set up a romantic evening to surprise her sweetheart when he got home.

She made shrimp cocktails, poured a couple drinks, lit candles, and put on some soft music and a sexy nightgown.

When Jim walked in after a long night at work, he said, "What's going on? Did the electricity go out or a circuit breaker go off?"

Michael and I have had our share of communication, or rather miscommunication, problems as well.

He asserts that there are four dreaded words a husband hates to hear: "What do you mean!" Especially when it's ended with an exclamation point rather than a question mark.

For example, recently I received a compliment from Jan's husband, Carl—in front of Jan—in regard to my diligent writing work habits. Before I could utter a thank-you, my friend blurted to her husband, "What do you mean! Are you saying *I'm* not disciplined?"

Or Michael will say something that he thinks is completely innocuous to me, and I'll respond, "What do you mean! Are you saying I'm _____ [fill in the blank: old? overweight? illogical?]." (All right, on that last one I'll have to concede.)

You know all those stereotypical dumb blonde jokes? Although I'm a brunette with a degree in journalism and several published books to my credit, I failed logic and could easily fit that stereotype in some areas.

For instance, when my book *Thanks for the Mammogram!* was translated into Spanish, I was excited to see it in another language—*Gracias por el Mamograma!* etc.—but also a little puzzled.

I showed it to Michael, who has studied Spanish, and

asked, "Honey, how come everything's in Spanish except for my name?"

"Because it's your name."

Ba-dum-bum. A prime example of Laura logic.

Part of the problem is that I can't be bothered with boring things like which way is north or how to use my cell phone, find my "cookies" on the computer (if they're not chocolate-dipped Oreos, I don't care), or do math.

When I was a newspaper reporter, part of my job included covering local government, which included a plethora of night meetings—city council, planning commission, school board, even cemetery district meetings (don't ask).

I would sit there and try to look interested as the board droned on and on about such scintillating subjects as zoning, permits, and the size of gravestones while scribbling away furiously in my reporter's notepad and afterward posing what I hoped were semi-intelligent questions to the board members.

Then I'd go back to the newsroom and type up my story.

I bluffed my way along pretty well for a while. But the day my editor gave me my performance review—"You're a wonderful writer, great at people stories, conscientious, and never miss deadline, but . . . you need to work on sharpening your governmental understanding a bit more"—I knew the writing was on the wall, so to speak.

A little later I quit and started writing humor books. For that you don't need to understand government. Unless you're Bill O'Reilly or Molly Ivins.

I also have miscommunication difficulties around anything involving numbers. Or mathematical concepts. Which is why Michael handles the checkbook.

That's why I'm always so surprised when people send me math puzzles or word problems on the Internet—especially people who *know* me. Why would I want to figure out a math problem? I HATE math.

Even more than peas.

It was enough that I finally graduated from college with a B in my bonehead math class—after failing the placement exam numerous times—but that's all behind me now. Why would I want to spend my precious time doing math for fun? *Fun* and *math* do not belong together in the same sentence.

The last time I thought of math as entertainment was when I saw the movie *A Beautiful Mind*, and then I was focusing not on the math—I glazed over during those parts—but on the wonderful love story.

For me, it's all about the story.

Here's a fun story about marital miscommunication from my friend Joyce in Ohio.

Her husband, Dan, was out working in the yard, so Joyce went to the back door to call outside to let him know lunch was ready.

Her: Weenies and beans!

Him: What kind?

Her: Weenies and beans.

Him: What kind?

Her: Twelve o'clock.

(If you can't figure out this marital miscommunication, go to the end of the chapter for the solution.)

Sheri, who's been married to Jim for more than twenty-five years, says she tries to hold her questions when her husband is talking. "I don't want to interrupt him," my sister-in-law said. "I just let him finish. My boss, Dave, has taught me a lot about communicating with men. He and I have had a few run-ins."

Most communication in a marriage is not necessarily verbal, Sheri asserts. "Being attentive counts more than what you would *say* about being attentive," she said. Sheri and Jim are fortunate, because they're both pretty accommodating people. "That makes it easier for us than most couples."

For instance, one day during her chemo treatments, Sheri was resting back in their bedroom and needed Jim to bring her something, but she doesn't like yelling through the house, so instead, she used her cell phone to call him in the living room with her request.

I tried that once with Michael, but it didn't work.

Since our house is relatively small, it was just as far for my husband to walk to get to the phone as it was for him to walk to my office to see what I wanted—which he let me know when he walked into the office with the phone to his ear.

Our Arizona friends Diane and Warren use a different approach to eliminate yelling through the house: walkie-talkies. "When he's in the den with the door closed watching his programs and I'm on the couch in the living room watching my programs, if we need to say something to each other, we use the walkie-talkies," Diane said. "Cheaper than cell phones."

Sheri and Jim went to a three-hundred-dollar marriage conference together once, and Jim is so tight-lipped that she said the only thing she found out about him is that he likes the toilet paper to roll over rather than under.

And that he doesn't like marriage conferences.

Unlike my friend Jan, who along with her husband, Mike, recently participated in a marriage group study with four other couples using a workbook called *Intimate Encounters* by Dr. David Ferguson.

"It really helped us in communicating with one another," Jan said. "When a spouse shares what's going on in his or her life, sometimes we may not listen. We just say, "Uh-huh, uh-huh," but to really listen, to take the *time*, makes a huge difference.

"Saying, 'Wow, it sounds like that really hurt you . . .' and acknowledging the person's feelings instead of offering an opinion or suggesting, 'You should have done this,' really helps. That really makes me know that Mike is listening to me, that he's understanding."

Lisa, my girlfriend who's been married to Hank for more than two decades, knows that she will never think the same way as her husband does, so she always jokes, "Whatever decision you'd make, Hank, think the opposite, and that's what I'd do."

Christie, a new pen friend who has a graduate degree in rhetoric and communication, is married to Greg, a stalwart Norwegian and a man of few words.

"In the first year of our marriage, I used to get really frustrated when I had something on my heart and I couldn't get much response from Greg," Christie recalled. "Pretty quickly, though, I realized how futile it was to start one of those really important discussions, just because I had been lying there stewing on it, at 10:30 at night. I've concluded that if a wife is trying to communicate anything other than a fire danger when her husband is sleepy, she won't get as much as a flickering eyelid."

Greg also explained to his wife that even though he sometimes wanted to tell her what he thought, he wasn't always sure exactly what he did think until he had pondered what she had said a little more fully. "Not everyone makes lightning-fast analysis of all the pertinent facts and comes up with twenty-four conclusions in the blink of an eye like you do, honey," her husband said. "Give me a minute—or thirty, will you?"

Sheri recalls a difficult time in her life when she was going through perimenopause, her twin daughters were in high school, and the house was always a mess. "It was a pigpen," Sheri said. "I lived with three pack rats who never picked up after themselves."

She communicated to her husband and daughters time and time again about the problem, but nothing seemed to change. Finally at her hormonal wits' end and unable to take it any longer, Sheri came to the conclusion that she needed a break—a place of her own for just a little while.

So she sat her husband down for a talk. "I really need to

go and get my own place for a while," Sheri told Jim. "I really need to be alone."

Jim, who's normally quite the joker, grew very serious and said plaintively to his wife, "Can I come too?"

❧

After Michael had his hernia surgery last summer, he had a four-week recuperation period during which he was limited in the things he could do—definitely no heavy lifting, pushing, or climbing.

Consequently, our backyard started looking a little scruffy, and I wanted to pitch in and help. So driving home from church one Sunday, I said, "Honey, how about if this afternoon you spot me on the ladder while I climb up and trim the branches on the plum-cherry tree that are hanging on the roof?"

My husband didn't think that was a very good idea.

"Darling, your coordination and balance really aren't the best," Michael said carefully. Then, trying to exercise some new communication principles we were trying to incorporate into our marriage, he said, "Would you say that's accurate or an insult?"

"No, it's not an insult," I huffed. "I just didn't think it was true."

"Honey, you've fallen and broken your arm three times. And that was on level ground."

"So what's your point?"

Then we looked across at each other and burst out laughing. No ladder climbing that day.

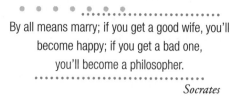

By all means marry; if you get a good wife, you'll
become happy; if you get a bad one,
you'll become a philosopher.

Socrates

Solution to Dan and Joyce's marital miscommunication puzzle: Dan thought Joyce was saying, "We need some beans," and the second time he said, "What kind?" she thought Dan was asking what time it was!

16

I Hope You Dance

One advantage of marriage, it seems to me, is that when
you fall out of love with him, or he falls out of love with you,
it keeps you together until you maybe fall in love again.

Judith Viorst

After years of marriage, most couples have reached a
nice easy comfiness in their relationship. But now
and then that comfort zone needs some revving up
with a little romance and passion.

189

And dancing. Especially cheek to cheek.

My sister-in-law is a big fan of dancing, especially around the house, to keep the romantic fires burning. "Put on a little music, start dancing, and see how long you can keep your clothes on," Sheri suggested.

After twenty-four years of marriage, Hank and Lisa have taken up ballroom dancing—now that the kids have finally left the house. The couple enjoys a little cha-cha, tango, and salsa dancing together once a week, which adds a little zing to the strings of their hearts.

I asked Hank and Lisa, and several other couples, what they do to keep the home fires burning in their household, as well as what helps to ensure a healthy, happy marriage, and they've given me permission to share their marital secrets:

Lisa, a fun, vivacious blonde, says she likes to do wild, off-the-wall things to keep her husband guessing. Like donning a brown wig on occasion to add a little mystery.

She recommends couples be crazy and unpredictable so their spouses never know what's going to happen. "That keeps the romance alive," Lisa said. "Hank always says, 'You never know what you're going to get.'"

Because her mom passed away last year after a long battle with brain cancer, Lisa also offers this important advice: "Don't take life too seriously. We're here for such a short time. Make sure you have a date night or time together—just the two

a kiss is still a kiss

of you; make sure to be spontaneous and always keep the other one wondering what you'll do next. Don't make it the same thing."

Sending cards and flowers is great, she advises husbands, but don't do it only on a typical holiday like Valentine's Day or anniversaries. Make it completely unexpected.

A husband sending flowers to his wife at work scores big on the romantic meter. Her female co-workers will all stop by her desk to ooh and aah and say, "Oh, he sent you flowers? You're so lucky. How romantic . . ."

"Guys don't realize how important that is," Lisa said.

I agree. But for the budget conscious, it can be a costly luxury. And wives know that. So an easy-on-the-pocket bouquet from the grocery store or some hand-picked flowers from the yard also work.

I must admit, though, that there's something about the utter impracticality and extravagance of the sent-flowers gesture that goes right to a woman's heart. It makes her feel cherished and valued that her husband would go to such an expense for her.

A suggestion, guys: start saving your pennies now so you can surprise her one day with this lavish gesture of love. Even if it's only once. You'll be amazed at how much it means to her.

And the nice rewards you'll reap.

After being married nearly half a century, my friend June tells me it's the little things that really make a difference: "tucking a love note in his lunchbox, baking his favorite apple pie instead of birthday cake (a candle in the center of the pie worked fine), lighting candles at dinnertime 'just because,' coordinating Friday lunch hours to share lunch, delivering a bouquet of red roses to me at home the day before I had surgery, spending evenings out—when we could afford it—and saying 'I love you' often."

Thoughtfulness is a key element to a happy, healthy relationship.

Sheri's husband loves a certain kind of almonds, as well as the large Spanish-stuffed olives, so she always makes sure her shopping trips include some for Jim. "I fill the house with stuff he likes."

In turn, Jim always brings home books and magazines his wife likes.

Jan and Mike enjoy spending time at home together. "We have a wonderful atmosphere with our gardens," Jan said, "and we enjoy using our backyard as a secluded getaway. We'll go out, start the barbecue, have some cheese and crackers . . ."

Since the couple doesn't have the funds at present to take off on a mini holiday, they enjoy the beauty close at home instead. "Just utilizing what God has already given us," Jan added. "Really enjoying each other and sharing the outdoors . . . talking and laughing, just being together. Just to talk, or enjoy each other's presence and *not* talk. Just being quiet with each other. Those things mean so much. Spending time just enjoying that person's presence is so valuable."

My brother-in-law Jim, a delivery driver with an early-morning route, calls Sheri, also an early riser, every morning at 4:00 from the road. If she isn't up then, he'll leave her a voice-mail message and she'll call him back. Jim leaves his sweetheart romantic voice-mail messages frequently. "He's always been good at that," Sheri said. "I sometimes save them."

TV in the bedroom can be good for a little amour too, the couple maintains. "A good movie and a little See's candy always lead to romance," Sheri said. "It started because I dropped some nuts and chews on my chest and he went after it. Things have never been the same since." (When I read this aloud to Michael, her brother, he said, "Too much information!")

My sister-in-law Debbie raves about her husband's thought-fulness to her. Married to a pastor, she was quick to share, "After a long, tiring day we'll get into bed, and he'll scratch my back for about thirty minutes or so. Then he wraps up with a short foot rub. And he does this almost every night."

Wow. That's better than a stint at the spa. Cheaper too, and she doesn't have to leave home.

Bob affirms to his wife how much he loves her and lets his fingers do the talking.

"After more than thirty years together, we appreciate each other, and 'show and tell' is our favorite pastime. Sometimes, as with the back scratching, no words are necessary," Debbie said. "Other times, he'll say something about how wonderful I am from the *pulpit*. There I am with a red face, but one glowing with appreciation. And I try to lift him up to others around me—how lucky I am, how much fun he is."

❧

Curt and Peggy have spent most of their thirty-two-year marriage in church ministry, and they've come up with a sweet and innovative way to express their love and appreciation to one another.

A few years ago, Curt bought a pretty blank journal and penned some encouraging and romantic sentiments to his wife, signed and dated the entry, and laid it on her pillow, where she'd be sure to see it.

When Peggy read her husband's tender words, she was moved to tears and took the time to write her own loving entry in return—and put it on Curt's pillow.

Now they know what to give the bride and groom who have everything: a blank journal as a wedding gift with this note tucked inside:

Dear [bride and groom],

A few years ago we began what we call our encouragement journal. We wanted to find a way to regularly express our appreciation to each other in writing, so we began taking turns writing notes to each other in a journal—dating each entry. When one of us finishes a note to the other, the journal is left open for the other to see, and they in turn write a note back.

Your journal can be used to express thoughts of love, appreciation, encouragement, admiration—anything that would bless the other. We try to be as specific as possible. We have had a lot of fun keeping our journal. Not only does it bless us as we read the notes for the first time, but it is wonderful to go back and reread notes from the past. We hope the two of you will be blessed with your own journal.

Margaret and Dan Saylar were married for forty-two years, and Margaret shared these wise marriage tips that they learned during those years:

Pray before marriage. My husband, Dan, and I prayed before we met. He prayed with me beginning with our first date, each date following, and each night after we were wed.

Take time to talk. One of the first things I noticed about Dan was that he was easy to talk to. We enjoyed discussing our mutual interests.

Appreciate your marriage partner. People were finding mates at a young age then, but we were older when we married. Dan was thirty; I was twenty-eight. We remember how lonely it can be when one is single.

Learn to be unselfish. The best advice we received when we married was given by our pastor. Give 60 percent and expect 40 percent. It's a paradox that by giving one receives. When we give attention to our spouses, it comes back to us. Jesus said, "Give away your life; you'll find life given back, but not merely given back—given back with bonus and blessing" (Luke 6:38 Message).

Maybe you've taken to heart some of these hints to spice up your marriage. I sure have. I'm making plans to enroll my beloved and me in a ballroom dancing class.

Fred and Ginger we may never be, but dancing cheek to cheek may be the start of something good.

If only I won't step on his toes too much.

There is no more lovely, friendly or charming
relationship, communion or company, than a good
marriage.

Martin Luther

Acknowledgments

My heartfelt thanks to all the people who shared their funny or poignant marriage stories with me: Cindy and Mark Akagi, Hank and Lisa Brys, Curt and Peggy Clark, Jan and Carl Coleman, Debbie and Bob Cullifer, Frank and Eve Dorf, Joyce and Dan Dingman, Jan and Mike Duncan, Dan and Ann Eickmeier, Rebecca and Waymond Fong, Pam Fortner, Sharon and Jim Hetland, Roanne and Ron Hobizal, Jim and Sheri Jameson, Mike and Rene Lewis, Tony and Marianne Lourick, Pat and Ken McLatchey, Dave and Dale Meurer, Steve and Chris Pond, Char Roushia, Margaret Saylar, Annette and Randy Smith, Christie Syftestad,

June Varnum, Lana and Michael Yarbrough, "Bill and Susie," "Don and Rachel," and "Jill and Frank."

Thanks once again to Lonnie Hull DuPont, Kelley Meyne, and all the great folks at Revell. And to my family, who puts up with me when I'm on deadline. But mostly to God, without whom none of this would be possible. Thanks, Lord, for being such a great matchmaker and bringing me my Michael. You knew just what I needed. You always do.

acknowledgments

Notes

1. Dave Meurer, *Daze of Our Wives* (Minneapolis: Bethany House, 2000), 69–70. Used by permission of the author.

2. Ibid., 25–26. Used by permission of the author.

3. Laura Jensen Walker, *Dated Jekyll, Married Hyde* (Grand Rapids: Revell, 2003), 81–82.

Laura Jensen Walker is the author of several humor books, including *Girl Time*; *God Rest Ye Grumpy Scroogeymen*; *Dated Jekyll, Married Hyde*; *Love Handles for the Romantically Impaired*; *Thanks for the Mammogram!*; *Mentalpause*; and *This Old Dump*, as well as the novel *Dreaming in Black and White*. A popular speaker and breast cancer survivor, she knows first-hand the healing power of laughter. She and her husband, Michael, live in Sacramento, California, with their canine "daughter," Gracie.

For information on having Laura speak at your event, or to learn more about Laura, please visit her website at www .laurajensenwalker.com. To write Laura, please email her at Laura@laurajensenwalker.com or write to her at P.O. Box 601325, Sacramento, CA 95860.

Hilarious and heartwarming

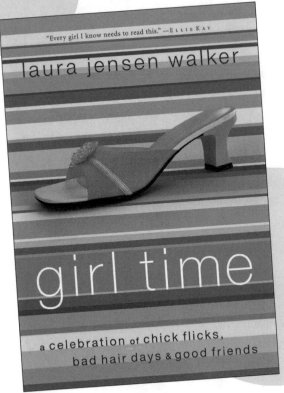

"Every girl I know needs to read this." —ELLIE KAY

laura jensen walker

girl time

a celebration of chick flicks, bad hair days & good friends

Girl Time. (n). A bonding ritual essential to females and indescribable to males, characterized by unmitigated chatter, sudden bursts of laughter, endless supplies of tissues, and chocolate.

books by **Laura Jensen Walker**

The process of a home makeover is challenging enough—let alone doing it side by side with your spouse! If you're an eager but beleaguered remodeler, you'll love *This Old Dump.*

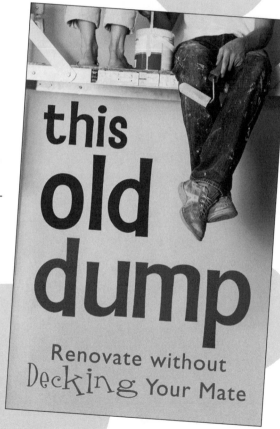

this **old dump**

Renovate without Decking Your Mate